The
MAGICAL
LANGUAGE
of the
HEART

The
MAGICAL
LANGUAGE
of the
HEART

REDISCOVERING
ANIMAL COMMUNICATION

DIANE SAMSEL

BUCHANAN BOOKS

Buchanan Books
PO Box 535
Tryon, NC 28782
info@BuchananBooks.com

ISBN-13: 978-0-9995430-6-1 (paperback)
ISBN-13: 978-0-9995430-7-8 (ebook)

Library of Congress Control Number: 2019948773
Buchanan Books, Tryon, NC

AstroDotBasic font by Robyn Clancy used with permission.

Any medical, psychiatric, or veterinary information in this book is for informational purposes only. The author of this book does not dispense medical, psychiatric, or veterinary advice, and this book is not intended as a substitute for the medical advice of physicians. The reader should regularly consult a physician in matters relating to his/her health and particularly with respect to any symptoms that may require diagnosis or medical attention.

Dedication

For Aunt Wimpy – Dorothy Tennessee Samsel. You validated my imagination and believed in me.

– and –

For Hans Picard – You are the rock to which I tether my spaceship. Your love of my uniqueness has sustained me for our thirty-two years together.

TABLE OF CONTENTS

LIST OF FIGURES

LIST OF TABLES

PREFACE

I am descended from a Southern tribe of storytellers. My father's ancestors came from Southern Germany, settled in Tennessee, and fought for the Union. My mother's South Carolina ancestors were a mix of English, Irish, and if you can believe 23andMe, Gold Coast Africans. I was raised mostly out west in California, where I was born, and in Oregon, where my father's parents settled after leaving Tennessee. Animals were always a part of my life growing up. We raised them as pets, tended them on the farm, hunted them in the forests, and fished from the streams and oceans. I was taught to be responsible for our pets and to *not* have feelings for all the others.

That last part was difficult for me. I have always felt a deep bond with all animals, experienced anguish when they were mistreated, and felt deeply ambivalent when they were harvested for food. As a child on my grandparent's farm, animals were food sources, and I had to harden my heart lest I be labeled a "city slicker," someone unable to deal with the harsh reality of a farm existence, and therefore unworthy of acceptance by that tribe. However, these same grandparents loved cats. They always had barn cats and one spoiled indoor Siamese.

My Southern relatives, by contrast, were totally urban and just a tad lazy but very social. The maids prepared most of the food. Prized animals tended to be of the hunting dog variety and never pets. There were one or two pet dogs scattered here and there, but those were usually pretty ill-tempered because my Southern relatives were not particularly warm-hearted people when it came to pets.

They were just hilariously funny people.

Their contribution to my upbringing came in the form of outrageous weekend parties that began Friday night with bourbon drinking, continued Saturday night with more bourbon and a fish fry (after a day of the men of the family fishing in the Congaree swamps), and capped off by Sunday dinners held after church around two in the afternoon. They resumed drinking immediately after church, and by the time we ate, the crowd was abundantly whisky-fueled and ready to tell and listen to stories. These celebratory weekend gatherings were where my family was the most enjoyable. The food was outrageously delicious, and the stories were wildly fun and brilliantly told, mostly by my grandfather, Daddy Earl. He saw humor in everything, a trait appreciated by much of that tribe, and that was the Southern family's saving grace: humor and the love of story. I inherited a solid work ethic from my Oregonian farmer grandparents (for which I'm eternally grateful), and I inherited my passion for story from my Southern relatives.

Because I was a child delivered by the stork to the wrong family, my sensitivity and empathic abilities were never appreciated or nurtured—much less valued—by anyone in my family. Except for my Aunt Wimpy. I think the stork that delivered her was the same one that delivered me. She saved my life by validating every out-of-the-ordinary part of my personality, especially my sensitivity. She believed in me. Sometimes it takes only one person to affirm a child. She was a miracle in my life.

I want to tell the story of my unusual journey of becoming an animal communicator, an astrologer, and more. There must be a lot of people who have had their sensitivities challenged by life's demands and who might appreciate hearing that, no matter how tough it gets, there is always the opportunity to become vulnerable once again and allow those sensitivities to blossom into a real talent. Talking with animals, listening to the language of stars and the planets—it's all possible and glorious if you allow it to happen. I wrote this book in part to provide a field guide for finding and developing your own inner specialness in a world that demands too much practicality and levelheadedness. This book is for all of the dreamers out there who in their heart of hearts know that the animals truly are talking with them.

ACKNOWLEDGEMENTS

My path to becoming an animal communicator began in the early spring of 1986. That's when Chief Two Trees came into my life and opened the door to a new perception, one that eventually reshaped my reality.

I would like to thank the teachers who have been important to me since that miraculous meeting in order of their showing up in my life: Chief Two Trees, Dr. Deborah Ooten, Beatrice Lydecker, Reverend Kate Bast, Noel Tyl, Kenn Day, Dr. Susan McClure, Penelope Smith, Dr. Paul Buchanan, Kathy Rose, and Elisabeth Grace.

My family—husband Hans Picard and daughter Monica Baltz—have been a source of support, fun, and inspiration during the writing process, cheering me on productive days and comforting me during writer's blocks and/or general meltdowns.

Special thanks go to my good friends Lucy Morris and Paula Sellers. They are a wellspring of inspiration in my life.

Thanks go to my contributors, and also to those who have allowed me to share their stories: Kim Caldwell, Katie Donovan, Elaine Keene, Tammy Kizer, Kelly McGowan, Kay Newman, Barbara Rawson, Kathleen Samalon, Margaret Sharon, Kristi Ullman, Heidi Vanderbilt, Anne (who is watching over Clyde), and Linda (you know who you are with your marvelous story!).

Thanks to the animals who have taught me: Buster, Deuk, the twenty-nine-year-old therapy pony at SIRE, Alligator, Sheeba, and Rusty. There are too many to mention really. I am humbled by their wisdom and am grateful to them all.

I want to thank Brad Buchanan, my publisher, for his wizardly talents in pulling my book into sharp focus. And thanks go to Robyn Clancy for use of the AstroDotBasic astrological font.

And lastly, thanks to Meg Atkinson and her beautiful mare Addy for their support (that's Addy with me in the cover photo).

THE JOURNEY

INTRODUCTION

"Until one has loved an animal, a part of one's soul remains un-awakened." –Anatole France

*L*earning the art of animal communication requires a fearless heart. I have had to overcome my fears of the *instinctual* world––having had to suppress my own instincts––to appreciate the power of the animals' world. That power comes from their ability to live completely in the present moment––of knowing they are complete and belong in their world. Humans, with their language-based self-knowledge, often become estranged from the natural world and lose their ability to understand that a powerful chthonic force binds all creatures on this earth.

There is a language encoded into this earthly force. This language is neither spoken nor written but arises naturally and is encoded into the very cells of the bodies that roam our planet. I would say that it is embedded into everything on the planet: people, animals, rocks, trees, bacteria, water…everything. That means everything lives and has meaning. To learn to speak with animals is to gain access to this universal language. Everyone has the code, and everyone can learn it.

The journey requires coming home to one's own animal body. The art of communication with animals begins to express itself when we humans honor our place in nature.

The Bible says we are here to have dominion over animals, and in general, we humans have taken that to mean having power over animals. This attitude has taken us away from respecting their lives to brutally using them as commodities (factory farms). Rather than "dominion," there is a more supportive translation of this word (and Bible scholars argue over the true intended translation): *Stewardship*. Stewardship implies that we have a God-given mandate to protect the animals in our care.

My vision for this book is to promote our stewardship of the living Earth. That's a tall order indeed, but like all visions, it begins with one insight. May this book serve to awaken that moment of insight that builds to the awareness that we can all communicate with the animals.

BEGINNINGS

I frequently mention that I believe anyone can learn the skills needed to effectively communicate with animals. Still, it certainly helps if you have a talent or at least an inclination to do so. Here I'm going to share with you some of my earlier experiences in life that should have been, for me, a big clue as to what my future had in store—experiences that led me to develop my intuitive skills and become an animal communicator. Perhaps these stories will help you discover your own big clue and motivate you to begin your personal quest to better communicate with animals.

My earliest animal-related memory is meeting Buster for the first time. Buster was a fluffy white kitten, and I was a very young girl. Buster didn't stick around long. I suspect he was just passing through to size me up. He must have decided I was too young to deal with at the time, but that I at least had potential. As it happens, Buster and I were destined for a relationship that would span decades.

I'll tell you more about Buster later, and how he was instrumental in convincing me that animal communication is real. For now, though, I'd like to begin my tale with the events that happened not long after I met Buster, events that opened my heart to animals while at the same time wrenching open my eyes to some of the more complicated aspects of our relationship with other occupants of this planet. And like many good stories, this one begins with a cow.

LEROY

Leroy was a Hereford calf born on my grandparents' ranch in Oregon and was my first close animal friend. My family moved from South Carolina to Oregon when I was seven. Dad had left the military as a lieutenant colonel after fighting in two wars and then joined Piper Aircraft as a salesman. His passion was flying airplanes. We settled in Hillsboro because that was his hometown as well as central to the location of his sales territory. His parents, Grandad and Grandma, owned a small "ranch" outside of the city limits, and that's where Leroy and I bonded.

My grandparent's property boasted a small herd of dairy cows, a filbert orchard, chickens, fruit trees, a rose and flower garden, and a large vegetable garden. They both worked hard from sunup to sundown, and their love and devotion showed in the tidiness, order, and health of the land, its buildings, and animals. The Samsel family excelled in two things: law and farming. Grandpa had been a sheriff, and his three brothers were attorneys. That branch of the family was mostly made up of hardworking, law and order folks. My grandmother was more playful, and from her side of the family, I inherited a sense of community and a desire to overfeed people. Grandma was a terrific cook. Her sugar cookies, made with lard, were amazing...sweet and savory. I digress.

Our family stayed at the ranch until we could find a house in town. Leroy had been separated from his mother and was living part-time in a stall in the barn and part-time outside, tethered in the middle of a scrumptious patch of rich green grass outside of the barn.

During our brief stay, Grandma tasked me with feeding Leroy. Several times a day, I would march from the farmhouse to the barn to feed him milk and calf feed, which were mixed in a bucket. Grandma taught me how to stick my hand down into the bucket and extend a few fingers so that Leroy would have a "nipple" with which to suck up his mash. At first squeamish, I soon learned that it was a pleasant enough task as Leroy loved his food. This is how we became such good friends. I had become his "mama" cow. After his meal, I spent time playing with him and currying his soft brown and white body. He exuded a fabulous baby animal smell like fresh grass and sunshine and earth. A little cow dung odor was thrown in for depth.

I was designated a "city-slicker" by my country cousins. They were veterans of ranch life and proud of their vast wisdom in the ways of nature. To them, I was a coddled hothouse orchid, and they delighted in teasing me about my vast ignorance of ranch matters. One such area where my ignorance showed was my understanding of the purpose of animals raised on a farm.

Leroy was naturally lonely, having been separated from his herd, and so was I. I had lived the first six and a half years of my life in South Carolina and left behind everyone I knew, including the tribal side of my family. I missed the great Sunday afternoon dinners with adults and children sitting for hours around the supper table talking, joking, and best of all—telling outrageous stories. I missed the Southern food: the fried chicken, fried okra, fried bream—the macaroni and cheese, butter beans, biscuits, and sweet potato pie. All served at the same meal. I missed the five desserts and the tea that was so sweet it could only be enjoyed served over a glass full of ice with a wedge of lemon to cut the sweetness. I missed the days of just hanging around on the veranda doing nothing but complaining about the heat and humidity. I missed the melting popsicles and the cooling afternoon monsoon rains.

In Oregon, I found myself living with pioneer people who knew how to do everything by themselves, and I was clearly out of my element. I had moved from *Gone with the Wind* to *Little House on the Prairie*. So it was with great naiveté that I allowed myself to bond with Leroy, to become his best friend—to lose my heart to him.

I was proud of my daily feeding chore. Each morning I would walk the path to the barn, past the little chicken house, the nut house (where the filberts were dried and stored after the fall harvest), and past the small fruit orchard to finally arrive at the big green barn where Leroy was tethered outside in the sunshine, standing in lush green late spring grass. Sometime in March, Oregon's endless weeks (sometimes months) of "liquid sunshine" gave way to beautiful, bright sunny days. I could not have felt better about myself on those first days spent on their ranch, getting to know Leroy and enjoying the creative outlets available to me.

I enjoyed currying Leroy, tending to his feeding, and playing with him. His favorite game was "head butting," which we enjoyed after his meal. I wore my dark brown hair in long pigtails and would arrive back at the house with the top of my head white with the hair from Leroy's forehead. Grandma laughed at this. It pleased me greatly that I could entertain her.

The ranch, at first, was a magical place. I had not yet encountered its harsher realities but would do so a few weeks later when I came for a visit (we had already moved into our new home and left my grandparents'), and Leroy was nowhere to be found. I stood in stunned silence when I saw the empty tether rope where Leroy had been tied up outside of the barn. I began to grasp the reality when I entered the dark and silent barn to see his stall empty. I ran to the barn door overlooking the pasture to see that Leroy was not out in the field. At that moment, I intuited that he was really gone and that I didn't want to know what had become of my friend.

It would be decades before I would process the grief I felt at that moment. I had been on the ranch long enough to begin to comprehend that the Samsel family were a bunch of stoics. My

Southern family enjoyed drama but not these Oregonians. So I clamped a little lid over my broken heart and said nothing. I knew better. Had I been back in South Carolina, I would have wailed for hours, making sure I had everyone's attention. Oregonians didn't put up with that.

Because most of us enjoy meat in our diets, we do not want to think about the beings from which it comes, much less be on friendly terms with them. I hid this early trauma way down inside myself, which made it hard for me to be close to animals for many years to come.

After my experience on the ranch, trees seemed like safer beings to me. I enjoyed and loved trees, and I learned to communicate with them instead. In Oregon, we had large stands of beautiful Douglas firs that still grew in virgin forests, and I loved to visit them with my family. I drew enormous comfort from trees, loving them with all my heart. I would go into forests behind my friends' houses, or near the farm, and climb into the trees and sit in total peace. I knew they welcomed me as much as I welcomed them.

When we moved to Newport Beach, California a few years later, the sycamore trees of Southern California became my friends. I loved the giant redwoods, but they seemed a bit distant. It was the sycamore that reached out to me. The Aborigines in Australia use sycamore trees for communicating long distances. This book is not about communicating with trees, but my journey has been about learning that communication is possible with all living beings. Each creature has a lesson to teach, and I love the trees for teaching me to trust. Their gift to me was providing a place of peace and comfort when I often experienced chaos in the world.

I was sensitive as a child, not easily understood, and I had few adults I could turn to for guidance. With young parents who were, in retrospect, big risk-takers, I must have seemed a burden with my high-strung and dramatic nature. Neither of my parents felt comfortable with my sensitivities. Slowly I became an outsider in my own family. But trees were solid and accepting, and so I talked with them, took comfort in their existence, and grieved when I learned of the logging of yet another virgin forest. Trees are deep, thoughtful, open, and opinionated beings. When I began to hone my talents later in life, I found that trees were great at giving advice on real estate! (But that's another story.) In my animal communication workshop, I've even assigned students the task of having a tree give them a poem! And the poems received have been beautiful.

BUSTER

It was Buster who pulled me out of my comfort zone with trees and opened up for me the world of animal communication. Animals reincarnate as do people and most beings on this planet. The soul is forever coming and going from spirit to form and back to spirit. Life is a cycle, and animals are comfortable with and aware of their place in the cycle.

Buster first came into my life when I was living with my family in Columbia, South Carolina, before we moved to Oregon. Dad had just gotten back from the Korean War, and it was our first Christmas together after his return. I don't know how this first little Buster came into my life, nor do I recall what his name was at the time, but we have a beautiful color slide of his tiny white fluffy kitten body climbing in our Christmas tree. Then he just vanished from my life. At age six, things like that happened to animals, and I never thought much about it—unless violence was involved. There were two rabbits Dad brought home for Easter that vanished from their cages, and I vaguely remember a story of the neighbor's boxer dogs being the culprits. I don't remember how I reacted to the news of these losses, but knowing my nature, it was probably melodramatically.

Buster next came into my life as a female cat I named Bippy. The year was 1962, and beatniks and coffee houses were very popular. "Bippy" was a popular slang phrase as in "You bet your sweet bippy." So I guess I named my kitty "ass." It was like me to not think things through back in those days. I just liked the sound of the word. A fluffy white gorgeous cat, Bippy completed the elegant look of my high school bedroom in Newport Beach. Mom and Dad had encouraged me to decorate it myself when I turned fourteen. So everything was lavender, purple, and white. I had a royal purple wall-to-wall shag rug, white satin bedspreads and skirts, and white organdy window treatments. I was inspired by those extravagant movie sets from the 1930s. Yikes! It's as if I had designed the room around Bippy's gorgeous long white coat. Her days were spent propped up, grooming herself against the purple, orange and blue throw pillows at the head of a twin bed. I liked Bippy, but I treated her more like a fashion accessory than as the friend she was. At the time, I was little more than a self-involved, neurotic teenager just beginning my career of hanging out with the wrong boys. I was too cool to get involved.

Dad died in a plane crash at the start of my sophomore year in high school. I was too emotionally immature to handle the loss of a parent, and Mom's grief left little room for my problems, so I went a bit wild over the next three years. I vented my grief by acting out and neglecting my studies, among other things. By my senior year, I had all but moved out of the house to live with my high school sweetheart (and bad boy) Lewis Baltz. That was 1962! What was I thinking! In California, I took it for granted that the world operated on the crazy rules I was inventing. Lewis and I later married, and altogether I spent seven years in that rocky, creative, fun, and disastrous relationship. From Lewis, I learned about art. He lived for photography even as a teenager, and our life together was a grand adventure. But it was a rocky time with him as we were always breaking up and coming back together.

Perhaps it was the emotional stress of my relationship with Lewis, but during our breakups, I bonded with Bippy as never before. Then, after graduating from high school, and another breakup from Lewis, my mom moved back to her home in Columbia, South Carolina. Bippy had been staying with Mom, and

I had no place to keep her, so I had to re-home Bippy, and to this day, I recall the unhappiness I felt at handing my friend over to strangers. But I had no skills in feeling much less processing grief in those days because I was a Samsel and therefore did not have feelings! I duly buried my remorse over Bippy as deep as I could. It would take years of therapy and a later encounter with Buster for me to finally excavate those feelings, learn to be truly human again, and to finally grieve the loss of my beloved and beautiful Bippy.

Buster/Bippy returned years later as Beauregard when I was in my twenties and married to Lewis. We had already separated but not divorced, and I adopted Beau as a kitten. He too was white but with one blue and one yellow eye and a little grey smudge on the top of his head. This is a cat breed called "odd-eyed whites." He saved my life a few weeks later when the apartment I was renting caught fire. Beau woke me up in time to alert my roommate and call the fire department. We were all safe as the fire was stopped before it blazed, and I thanked Beau for his bravery. Sadly, he was perhaps a little too brave. He could go outside whenever he wanted, and years later, he was taken by foxes near our home on the outskirts of town.

After graduating from college in 1979 with a BFA in studio painting, I moved to Houston Texas and worked for a small consulting firm that put together museum-quality art for big corporate clients. Near my apartment, under a car parked at the neighborhood gas station, I found a small, white kitten with one blue and one yellow eye and a small smudge on the top of his head. I fell in love and felt his kinship immediately. It was the return of Beauregard!

A woman I worked with had a son named Buster, and her devotion to her son impressed me. In honor of my co-worker's son, I named the new kitten Buster. He remained with me up until the time, many years later, I launched into my shamanic studies.

Buster was to teach me to trust my deep bond with animals, and I gave my heart completely to the little guy.

At the end of Buster's life, his death left me bereft for weeks. This was an extreme reaction for me, and I think it was in part because his death brought into focus so many prior losses that I had never properly grieved—Leroy, Bippy, Beauregard, my father . . . . The dam had finally burst, and as a result, my heart began to heal.

Not long afterward, I began my career as an animal communicator. I had been in touch with Buster in spirit and knew he was ready to return and resume our path together. He let me know he wanted to be a big cat and suggested a Maine Coon. I found a breeder I liked and gave her a call. She told me she had no kittens at the time, which was okay with me as I wasn't quite ready myself. Some months later, I had a dream in which Buster One came to me and said, "I'm being born." The dream ended in a brilliant flash of white light that woke me up. As soon as it was appropriate to call, I dialed the breeder. She greeted me with a cheery, "I've been up all night delivering kittens!" I wanted a boy. She sent photos of twin kitties that looked like tiny pink fluff balls, and I said send me one, trusting that Buster's spirit would inhabit the kitten I received.

Four months later, Buster "Two" arrived. He was a pale pinkish-orange with a silver undercoat and pale orange stripes with copper tips—his beauty swept me off my feet. And he arrived with the confidence of a prince.

Hans and I had three other cats at the time—Serena, Rusty, and Cookie. Buster, even though only four months old, outweighed them and was roughly their size. Upon meeting them all, he launched a charm offensive, and we never had one cross word from any of our cat family. We all fell in love with him on sight.

Till his death seventeen years later, Buster communicated with my clients, sitting alongside me in my office while I was on the phone. When he died in 2014, I grieved as though I had lost a family member. I gave Buster a beautiful funeral with candles and flowers and soft guitar music. The cats in the house were able to pay their respects, and Buster was able to adjust to being a spirit once again.

AWAKENING

Even before I became an animal communicator, I was always interested in all forms of communication, both verbal and otherwise. Along with studying painting, I also later developed an interest in making videos. Friends of mine from those college days, Anna Benson and Mark Henriksen, had been artists who, as a married couple in the '80s, developed the *Firm Workout* video exercise series that showcased their wonderful creative talents. During college, I had starred in Anna's graduate school video. Sadly, that video was lost in the mail and never recovered. Mark also availed himself of my acting talents. He put me in the role of the scolding wife heard in the background of *Miss Dolph*, his fine arts film about an elderly woman in crisis.

I became professionally involved with video in the summer of 1986. That's when I accepted a position working at a small video production company in the role of sales, scriptwriter, and video producer. The company, Video Marketing, was started by fine arts photographer Scott Trees to take advantage of his state-of-the-art video production studio in Black Mountain, North Carolina. Scott is considered one of the top equine marketing photographers in the world. His photographs of million-dollar horses are much in demand worldwide. Video marketing, however, focused on industrial videos, and Scott hired me to develop their industrial client base.

I wore many hats in Scott's little company and loved the work. At my desk at 8 a.m., I stayed on the phone until I landed an interview with a company. I would drive to the appointment and work with the company to produce a sales or training video.

Once I secured the contract, I'd conduct interviews and design a script. Once the script was approved, I would participate in the production of the video, which involved managing the shooting and editing of the finished product. It was my dream job. During that summer I met my husband, Hans, and together we bought our first home across the street from Trees Photography there in Black Mountain. It was heaven!

And here is where the plot thickens.

Scott and his wife at the time, Lois, both enjoyed a close friendship with Chief Two Trees, a Cherokee tribal council chief and medicine man who lived nearby. I had heard of Chief Two Trees from Scott and others who worked at Trees Photography and was a bit afraid of him because the stories of his intuitive powers seemed so otherworldly and strange. Chief ran a "clinic" on his property in Old Fort, NC. A large gallon jar stood on the railing of the porch of his unpainted house deep in the woods. In that jar, Chief's "patients" placed donations following their visits with him. He would sit down across from a visitor, take a long slow look, and then proceed to diagnose physical and psychological ailments.

One hot summer day in late June, Chief Two Trees came into my little cubicle workspace and sat down on a chair directly in front of my desk. It was my first encounter with the great man. He stared at me with his huge dark eyes for a few moments until I had no choice but to give him my full attention. What happened next changed my life forever. Chief Two Trees began to give me my first teaching. That teaching was the first of several important lessons that laid the foundation for my work as an intuitive.

The redirection of my life initiated by Chief Two Trees came just before a planned move out of state. Hans works as a consultant, and we had already committed to moving to Cincinnati, Ohio for Hans to assume management of a project at a large power plant on the Ohio River.

Still, after our move, I was determined to follow up on my awakening as an intuitive. I began to read everything I could on the subject of shamanism. I gobbled up the books of Carlos Castaneda. I seized an opportunity to study with Kenn Day, the author of *Post-Tribal Shamanism*, in his workshops. When possible, I traveled back to Old Fort to continue mentorship under Chief Two Trees. Having read about shamanism, I was curious as to the extent of Chief's powers. On one visit with him at Old Fort, I asked him if it was true that shamans can be in two places at the same time. He then told me the story about being seen in two places on the same day. He said he was in London, England on business but had to sign important legal papers back in the States. Witnesses told him that he appeared at the office and signed the legal papers, although Chief told me he was in fact in London at the time.

On one visit with Chief Two Trees, he had just completed building his new clinic in Old Fort and wanted to show me around. It was a cold autumn evening in the mountains, and his clinic still had construction material scattered around the bare earth surrounding the building. We entered a side door, and I walked into a dark room. Before he could turn on the lights, I saw a brilliant array of Indian chiefs seated around a circular fireplace. When the light was thrown, the room appeared white and empty. The circular fireplace was cold, and no one sat around it. Feeling shaken at what I had seen, I asked Chief about it. He laughed and said that the chiefs I saw often met there, and it was not anything to be alarmed about. They enjoyed his council fire! Such was his magical world. I had to go back to Cincinnati and my day job and integrate this magic into my ordinary life. It wasn't easy. Chief's words opened up startling new dimensions for me, and I cherish his memory.

The next major wake-up call in my life occurred in 1992 when Beatrice Lydecker came to Cincinnati to hold animal communication sessions for the public. At that time, she enjoyed quite a bit of fame as an animal communicator, appearing on Oprah Winfrey and Johnny Carson's shows. I had read one of her books, *What the Animals Tell Me*[1], and was willing to take the plunge, so

I took two of my cats, Buster and Serena, to meet her. When we met, she told me that Buster wanted to know what had happened to the houseplants. Buster loved his houseplants, and I had just moved them outside for the summer. That simple comment from Ms. Lydecker convinced me animal communication was real.

More evidence of the effectiveness of animal communication came about a year later when my six-month-old Siberian husky, Sara, was stolen from a dog run that attached to our home. We had installed a door for her and her brother, and they could go outside any time they wished. We had a ten-foot-high fence around the run with a locked gate to keep them secured and safe. However, one early Saturday morning around 2 a.m. someone climbed over the fence and stole Sara.

Her brother, Cutter, had been in the pen with Sara, and it was his barking that awoke the household. I rushed downstairs to find Sara gone from the pen. Losing her felt agonizing.

In an effort to recover Sara, I employed two communicators—Donna Zimmerman and Chris Celek. Although they each told me seemingly conflicting stories, it turned out that both stories were correct. Donna accurately described the twenty-year-old man who climbed over the fence and stole her, and Chris described the family he had given her to a few weeks later. I spent a week distributing a thousand professional "Lost Dog" posters (from pet detective Sherlock Bones) within a four-mile radius of our home. One of those posters miraculously landed on the bulletin board of a bowling alley in another town about five miles away from us. A patron, in for his Wednesday bowling league, saw Sara's poster and realized his new dog belonged to someone who was looking for her.

When Sara was returned, her rescuer told me the story: He and a friend were enjoying a beer at the bar after his bowling league meet when his friend drew his attention to the bulletin board and remarked, "Isn't that your dog?"

The rescuer and his family returned Sara to me the very next day.

They were upset to discover she had been stolen. The thief worked at a fast-food restaurant where the rescuer's son also worked part-time. I later learned that the thief had been attending a party in our neighborhood and had decided, in his inebriated state, that it would be fun to steal a dog. Once sober, he quickly realized that a Siberian husky puppy was not so easy to keep. He ditched Sara by giving her to his younger co-worker at the fast-food restaurant, who was thrilled to have such a prized puppy.

The rescuer's son provided me with the perpetrator's name and phone number. I had reported Sara's theft to the police earlier and so had an open case. The police went over and arrested the man for being in possession of stolen goods. That felt so satisfying. It had taken me a month to get Sara back. It was an effort that consumed a significant amount of personal effort and money, all the while dealing with mounting anxiety and grief.

The two animal communicators who helped me were spot-on in their assessments of what had happened to Sara. I was grateful to them, of course, but I was also greatly impressed by them, and the entire experience inspired me to become a good communicator myself—especially one who helped locate lost animals.

AND SO IT BEGINS

Sometime late in 1997, my friend Lucy Morris called to invite me to join her in attending a four-hour workshop on animal communication to be delivered by communicator Kate Bast. A few years earlier, before she became a professional communicator, I had worked with Kate on a project at my home and had enjoyed listening to her carry on conversations with my animals. She clearly delighted in communicating with them, and I loved hearing the conversations. Her workshop was no less entertaining. She gave us a bit of instruction and then set us loose to try communication on our own.

Those first communications proved incredibly satisfying and easy for me. The goal of the workshop was to have each student talk with an animal (looking only at a photo) and receive some information that the student could not have known. I looked at the photo given to me by my practice partner of a horse and immediately picked up the horse's digestive issues. I became energetically in tune with the horse and felt the tightness in her stomach. I burped in response to studying the photo. Using the simple techniques Kate taught, I was able to focus on the horse in such a way that I immediately felt what was going on in the mare's digestive tract. My partner was able to confirm this observation as being accurate. I learned that being able to feel what another being feels is called empathetic communication, and it is one of the four basic ways we communicate non-verbally. If you're the type of person who can pick up such things as headaches from other people, you are probably highly empathetic.

I left the workshop and eagerly tested my skills with anyone who would allow me to experiment with their animals. After a few months, I felt I was good enough to enter the field professionally. My first call was from a woman in Lexington, Kentucky, an hour's drive away. During the call, she expressed concern about her Belgian mare she had rescued from a kill pen the previous year.

Lexington is the home of thoroughbred racing. There are many farms breeding thoroughbred horses in the area. It is standard practice that as soon as the thoroughbred babies are born they're removed from the mothers and taken to another farm and given to a Belgian, who becomes the little foal's surrogate mother. The Belgian would have been bred at the same time as the thoroughbred, and her foal would be taken from her shortly after birth to be sold for slaughter. Many fashion items are made with the hides of these little guys. It's a rough industry, and that's why I do not like the sport. Certain farms in the area specialize in these Belgian herds, and the horse I traveled sixty miles for and charged $25 to visit for an hour came from such a farm.

The mare's name was Blue, and when she was rescued, she was carrying little Happy, a foal born shortly after her rescue. My human client called to say that Blue was acting extremely nervous—she felt something was wrong. (I have changed names here as I have lost track of these clients).

On an overcast and chilly fall day, I arrived at the farmhouse quite a distance from the city. The house, located off of a tiny farm road, was somewhat dilapidated with paint peeling from the sides of the building, and in the backyard there was a deerskin thrown up into the bare branches of a large tree.

My human client, a cheerful woman in her late forties, small, neat, and dressed in jeans and a sweatshirt, took me out to the barn—a ramshackle affair put together with what looked like random pieces of wood and painted various shades of red. Several unpainted sheds stood (or leaned) scattered around the property. Blue was in the paddock, and I stood on the opposite side of the fence to talk with her. Her enormous body twitched with anxiety, and she gave me an unsettled look. I could tell right away that she felt terrible about something. I stood on my side of the fence, not knowing if I could trust Blue.

I began the communication by asking Blue about her concerns. I explained how her person had recognized that she was troubled by something and had called me to come over to talk about what her concerns might be. Blue wasted no time and began by pointing her enormous head in the direction of what she said was a den full of coyotes and that she knew coyotes kill babies—she was terribly concerned for the safety of her foal, Happy. I relayed this information to my client, and she confirmed that there was a den in that direction and she knew about it. She told me that they weren't coyotes though, they were coydogs—a mix of feral dogs and coyotes. These particular coydogs were much bigger than coyotes and so much more threatening to the horses. She told me to tell Blue that she'd get a donkey for the pasture (donkeys will kill a coyote in a heartbeat).

Blue visibly relaxed when given this assurance. I asked if there was anything else worrying her. She told me (through pictures, a few words, and thoughts) that men were coming in the night with big bundles on their backs and putting them into one of the weathered outbuildings near the barn. And then, to my great surprise, Blue said, "Drug dealers are dangerous!" I paled a bit and hesitated to pass on this little bombshell. At that moment, it occurred to me that Kentucky's biggest cash crop at the time was marijuana. I wondered: Was my client and her husband growing the crop? If so, were they dangerous? Were the men storing sacks at night hiding big bales of pot in those sheds? That was at the height of the war on drugs, and getting caught was serious. Everywhere you went in Kentucky, DOJ men could be seen in black cruisers or eating at restaurants off the interstate. Had Blue just busted her people?

I took a deep breath and, apologizing for the strangeness of the information, blurted it out. My client turned pale. *Uh oh*, I thought. She paused, put her head down, thought for a moment (I was holding my breath), and then said, "That's incredible!" Then she proceeded to tell me the story of how the year before horse thieves had arrived in the middle of the night with a trailer and stolen all of her horses except Blue. She said the men were captured shortly afterward and jailed. Her horses were returned, but Blue had been anxious during the ordeal and remained anxious ever since. In his confession, the thief had admitted leaving Blue behind because she was too big for the trailer. My client concluded this story by saying, "And he was this area's biggest drug dealer!"

At that point, she was crying and hugging Blue's enormous neck, and Blue was hugging her back. She continued stroking her neck and assured her that the bad man was in jail and would never scare her again. When it was time to leave, I said goodbye to Blue. She walked over to where I stood at the fence and leaned her enormous head down to mine. She gently touched her forehead to mine and beamed a brilliant white light of gratitude into me. The energy of that light nearly knocked me off my feet. Words cannot describe the magnitude of that blessing. I will never forget her. A week later, my client called to say that Blue, Happy, and the new donkey were in the pasture relaxed and enjoying their lives.

My career as an animal communicator had begun.

THE
FUNDAMENTALS

*C*ommunication between humans and other life forms on this planet goes back to the dawn of our species. Tribal cultures worldwide traditionally have assigned one or more of their group the role of interpreter for the non-human parts of the world. That person was usually given the title of shaman, or medicine man (woman). American Indians believed that everything on Earth possessed a spirit whose voice could be accessed by the shaman.

Imagine our ancestors gathered around a fire under a clear, starry sky on a moonless night. The seasons are slowly shifting from the warmth and abundance of summer to the chill of fall. The tribe feels fear mingled with excitement and turns as one to the individual they trust to interpret the mystery of their universe. He has talked with the great tusked wooly mammoth, the cave bear, and the crane. They tell him of their preparations for the coming winter. They explain how they know to store layers of fat or to grow extra fur or fly south for better fishing. Under the vast darkness, the shaman weaves a story from the natural world, pointing to the sky and the stars. He casts the shapes of the animals into the brightest stars, pointing to a constellation and asking his tribe to believe that there in that vast dome of darkness is the Great Bear. The shaman comforts them with the Great Bear's story about the coming of the cold weather.

I have been an animal communicator now for over twenty years. I've come to believe that sharing communication with non-human entities is something that anyone can learn. I've taught classes for most of those twenty years and find that students are able to pick up the skill of inter-species communication easily. I believe it is an innate talent humans possess. We humans are animals too. I like the term "featherless bipeds," a humorous term first used by Plato somewhere in the fourth century BCE. Our cultural training demands that we become "language dominate" and in so doing we have to set aside our intuitive skills of interpretation. Our reliance on the spoken and written word defines us as a species in so many ways. However, our intuition and imagination can be developed to just as fine a degree as our other communication skills.

The human body is an instrument of tremendous sensitivity. Each cell in our body has its own awareness and receives, energetically, ongoing and subtle messages from everything the body is exposed to in life. With training and awareness, it's possible to receive and interpret information coming through many non-verbal channels.

Willingness and awareness comprise the two keys to success in communication of any type. Once you become willing, by suspending doubt and self-judgment, the awareness needed to respond to the subtle, non-verbal signals that abound in your world naturally arises.

Since you are reading this book—and, in particular, this section of the book—I think we can reasonably stipulate your willingness to be a participant in animal communication. So here I'm going to begin with your awareness and how you can maximize your sensitivity to the energies around you. Awareness starts by being grounded, and by "grounded," I mean the term in practically every sense of the word: physically, spiritually, and mentally. Let's explore that.

FEET ON THE GROUND

In my early adulthood, I was never well-grounded. My mind could be as easily distracted as a dog's when he sees a squirrel. I'm a dreamer, an artist, and a creator. Animals dream and have incredibly creative experiences too, but animals always have their feet—or bellies—on the ground. Fish swim in the water, but they're always energetically in touch with where they are at any given instance. Birds fly in the sky, and they always know where they are and where they're headed. Why do humans have such a difficult time with being grounded? We drive down the interstate and wonder why we failed to notice that we just zipped by our exit. Our minds often seem locked in mental feedback loops that distract us from noticing our exact physical location on Mother Earth. I was one of the worst. Even in the third grade, teachers would send notes home to my parents: Diane does not pay attention! I was in a daydream. I was anywhere but in my body. It took me decades to learn to ground myself.

I think the reason for this lies in our education. As our civilization advances with technology, our physical actions shape our daily lives less and less. As young children, we are trained away from using our intuition as we become language and writing dominant. We are told that our invisible friends are "just our imagination" or that the cat did not say she wanted more tuna even though we, as children, hear the cat ask for tuna. Adults, in their busyness, ignore the rich and fantastic styles of communication that children naturally express. I knew what Leroy the calf needed and read his loneliness and his desire to have a friend. But I could not share this wonderful knowledge with anyone without being told I was making it up.

So what has this to do with having our feet on the ground?

Humans in "civilized" situations spend more and more time in thought processes as they mature. The natural ground under most people's feet is paved over in some manner. We wear hard, insulated surfaces on our feet. We go from one air-conditioned situation to another. Heat bothers us, cold bothers us, and even the wind bothers us. We spend a lifetime defending against experiencing nature. We spend a lot of time in our heads, in other words, and little time in the dirt.

As a result, humans living in modern civilization have lost the grounding ability that comes naturally when feet are exposed to dirt. There is a strong energy that comes up from the Earth, and all animals use that energy to survive. It comes up through the feet and informs and protects the body.

Yes, Mother Earth communicates too—through her energy field. There are well-researched scientific studies available on the internet describing how birds migrate, how lost cats travel hundreds of miles to find their people, and how whales in the ocean communicate over vast stretches of water. Aboriginals can go out into the wilderness by themselves and thrive for months at a time just by being open to all the information coming from the land and its inhabitants. And some enlightened humans have used their connectedness with nature to bring us marvelous information. Botanist George Washington Carver revitalized the economy of the South when he introduced crop rotation. He invented hundreds of products using peanuts and sweet potatoes. When asked how he knew so much about what his plants could do, he is said to have replied, "The plants tell me what they do."

GROUND YOURSELF BY GETTING CENTERED

It's estimated that humans process tens of thousands of thoughts a day, and most of these thoughts are similar thoughts from the previous day. Staying in the present and being in the authentic moment can be difficult for us. Through the practice of yoga and meditation, we can drift on the stream of thoughts rather than being commanded by them. When you are able to rise above this torrent of thinking, you can get into a space that is much more natural for the body. It's in this quiet space that your body becomes an instrument for receiving the information being communicated by other forms of life cohabiting our planet. I also work as an astrologer and believe that the Sun, Moon, planets, and stars are also in communication with us. These heavenly bodies have their own energy interacting with ours day in and day out. Intuition and imagination are our innate abilities that enable us to assimilate and decode the information streaming by us and through us from this living environment we call Earth.

I think of intuition as spontaneous and effortless insight and knowing. And to me, imagination is the childlike ability to know that there is truth in what your heart is telling you. As such, intuition and imagination working in concert become the instrument you will use to tune into the universe's conversation.

But the power you will use to successfully join that conversation is *intention*. Animal communicators avoid "trying to communicate" and make it a practice to "intend" to communicate. Effort implies will, and willpower is ego-driven —and both are key elements of intention. There's a lot more to be said about intention. For a good read on the subject, I suggest Wayne Dyer's book: *The Power of Intention: Learning to Co-create Your World Your Way.*

As you open the door to communication, it's important to keep in mind that animals can only communicate about the present moment because they live exclusively in the present. Horses grazing in the field are in a state of deep meditation. They're not thinking about their next dental appointment. Cats sunning for hours on end seeming to gaze into infinity are enjoying the bliss of being in the moment, processing nothing more than the energies that make up our world. Even when they're focused on survival issues, they become one with their environment, knowing instinctively what they're meant to do. Every part of the animal is open to sensory data, and they use their brains to make sense of it.

Animals are smart. It seems that every year new research shows that animals are much smarter than we previously thought possible. Frans de Waal, one of *Time Magazine*'s hundred most influential people, is a scientist and professor at Emory University. He is the director of the Living Links Center at the Yerkes National Primate Research Center. He's written a wonderful book: *Are We Smart Enough to Know How Smart Animals Are?*[2] I highly recommend this book for a more in-depth understanding of how the animal mind and psychology work. It is a highly compassionate, informative, and enlightening book that is reshaping how science views the animal mind.

By comparison, modern humans are not gifted at living in the moment and have developed the habit of living with complex mental defenses. For instance, when meeting a new person, we acknowledge them with a smile, a handshake, maybe a few chosen socially adept comments. In our own minds, though, we're often running a conversation that is keeping us from acknowledging the uniqueness of the person we're meeting. We fail to hear their words because we are busy thinking of what we want to say in response. People are seldom fully receptive mentally to what the other person is communicating. Maybe we're judging that person. Maybe we're criticizing something about our own appearance. Our social habits often prevent us from being authentic. To counter this habit, we need to learn to stay in dialogue with others, that is, to respond to what others are saying in a way that builds on a conversation. It's the same when we first talk with animals. The key is to stay in a dialogue. To ask questions, to clarify, to inquire. And at the heart of this skill, we must suspend judgment. To become comfortable in this natural space, we first must learn to ground ourselves in the truth of what we are hearing from others.

Grounding the body begins the process of communication. Placing the feet on the ground, standing or sitting still, and feeling that connection with the earth. In my workshops, I lead the group in a grounding exercise at the very start of the session, right after introductions are made. I can feel the energy settle down as people go from the excitement of thinking about what they'll be doing in the workshop to actually having their first physical experience of being in the energy that facilitates animal communication. I've been using the same exercise for almost twenty years—here is what we practice:

Begin in a seated position, eyes closed, back straight. Both feet are on the ground. Take a few deep breaths, relax the shoulders, smile inwardly, and then imagine a white light entering the toes of the right foot. Imagine bringing the white light slowly through the small bones of the toes, across the larger bones of the foot's arch, finally anchoring it in the heel bone. Now do this on the left foot. Imagine the light slowly moving through the bones of the left foot. Then imagine bringing that white light up from the heel to the ankle of both feet, to anchor in the ankle. Slowly bring the light up through the shins of both legs to anchor in the knees. From the knees, imagine the light traveling up to the hips. Anchor the light in the hips. Feel the warmth of the light in your hips. From the hips, slowly bring the light up the spine, the neck, and the skull.

I always end this exercise telling my students they can open their eyes on the count of three. Always come out of this grounding exercise slowly and mindfully. At this point in our workshops, everyone is relaxed and grounded enough to start working with animals, to allow their entire body to be used as a receptor.

THE STORY OF ALLIGATOR

I'm often asked what is the most unusual animal I've talked with in my career. I have to say that Alligator is up there near the top. This reptile can live over fifty years, weigh up to a thousand pounds, and reach a length of fifteen feet! The species has been around for about 150 million years and outlasted the dinosaurs, which died out 65 million years ago. Alligator taught me an early lesson in how communication is tied to the energies of the Earth.

The low country around Charleston, South Carolina names a land steeped in a rich culture of beauty and mystery. It is a landscape of thousand-year-old oaks, marshes, swamps, and the alligator. As yet, the creeping encroachment of man-made development has failed to tame this ecology of spartina grass and alligator filled creeks. Charleston's long history is filled with American aristocrats, pirates, voodoo priestesses and priests, slaves, great fortunes as well as great losses and sorrow. To anyone who comes to love the area though, the alligator is the one fact of life that demands as much respect as the dangerous hurricanes that blow through Charleston during the hot and humid summer season.

We once owned property on Dewees Island, a barrier island forty-five minutes from downtown Charleston (accessible only by ferry). Ten minutes into the ferry ride from Charleston a primitive world unfolds, allowing a communion with nature not available to most Americans. Dewees development began in the 1980s as this country's first ecologically sustainably developed real estate project. The island's 1,200 acres has 800 set aside for wildlife. All development, including roads, is confined to the remaining 400 acres. The roads are sand, and no cars are allowed; people who live there get about on golf carts, and there is a 17 mph speed limit! Houses cannot landscape with anything but plant species native to the island. Tucked inside the maritime forest, the majority of the houses are hard to see and are kept below five thousand square feet to assure that McMansions don't dominate the island.

Scattered around the interior of the island are small ponds. Alligators have made some of these ponds their homes. Dewees personnel train humans to avoid all interaction with the animals—for the safety of humans and alligators. A human who feeds an alligator teaches the alligator to be aggressive with humans, dooming the life of the animal. When Hans and I kayaked on the creeks that run between the acres and acres of marsh and spartina grass, it was not uncommon to come face-to-face with an alligator going the opposite direction.

Several years ago, I held an animal communication workshop on the island to raise money for the local seabird rescue group. At the end of the last day, we were invited to sit on the broad screened-in porch of a home overlooking a big pond. The pond was home to a twelve-foot bull alligator. Our assignment for that portion of the workshop was to communicate with this ancient being.

The students called forth all the techniques they had learned during the workshop and earnestly began to communicate with Alligator.

In my communication, I asked the alligator to please show me what it was like to live in the mud. What I got back from him cannot easily be put into words because the experience was so vastly different from anything I had experienced with human cognition. I shared with the students that it felt like what I imagine a psychedelic trip in a mud bath would feel like! I experienced a feeling of being grounded that was beyond description, like I was mud itself, and within that sensation, I experienced a riot of beautiful colors. Alligator told me that those were the beautiful "thoughts" that they enjoyed all day. These "thoughts" had no relation to the world as we organize it but more to a primal world. They were like visual drumbeats. Alligator assured me that they felt "delicious" and that they enjoyed a new thought with each heartbeat. I emerged from the experience quite disoriented.

I asked Alligator what he had to teach me, and he answered: survival. He said he has survived because he is more like Earth, more than any creature. He says his heart beats with the heart of the Earth, and that is how he has survived.

Hans is a scientist. He was in the workshop that weekend and buddied up with another man, an attorney (whose wife "made" him attend the workshop!). These two men "humored" us and did quite well in the exercises. But I could tell they weren't as engaged as we all were . . . until we talked with Alligator. Hans became very animated talking about his experience. He said Alligator let him inside of his body, and he got to experience Alligator's hunger and humor! Hans asked the alligator what he liked to do and with great dramatic flair told us in a deep and throaty voice that Alligator told him, "I like to eat!!!"

But the amazing thing to my scientist husband is that Alligator showed him how to "call" alligators.

Hans and I visited Brookgreen Gardens shortly after this workshop. Brookgreen Gardens is located about ninety miles north of Charleston and is one of the most wonderful nature spots on the coast. Built on a former rice plantation (the house no longer stands), Brookgreen has a beautiful sculpture garden and a wildlife center that features an alligator enclosure built around a natural creek. We stood above a creek admiring a small alligator sunning itself below us on a patch of grass. Although no words were spoken, I could tell that Hans was "calling" the alligator; I watched it slowly turn around and come towards him. I turned to look at Hans and saw the look of delight on his face. Just at that moment, there was a huge commotion in the shallow creek below her. An enormous bull alligator emerged from under the mud and charged Hans. Luckily a fence separated us from the creek! Hans looked at me and said, "Must be his girlfriend I was calling!"

Hans explained to me that his first alligator interaction taught him to communicate with the limbic system, the portion of the brain that is located at the base of our skulls. He said Alligator told him to send thoughts and energy out with this portion of the brain, and they would hear him and respond.

Now, whenever we are around wild alligators, Hans can make them respond by calling them. Seeing a wild alligator respond to human psychic communication is one of the more profound and thrilling experiences in my career and drove home for me the importance and effectiveness of being grounded.

Being grounded with the body is essential to this work. The energy of the Earth must flow freely up through our bodies in order to connect with the creatures, plants, and minerals that exist on this planet with us. We humans are from the earth and our bodies will return to the earth. All creatures know this instinctively. Humans have many defenses against sharing these sensations. One of my favorite gripes is the extreme high-heeled shoes worn by so many women. Setting aside the damage this does to the alignment of the spinal cord, it keeps the foot from being grounded. This fashion accessory alone removes the body from a free-flowing source of vitality that our animal bodies crave. As a communicator, I've had to pay attention to footwear that helps me keep my feet on the ground!

The best grounding comes from walking barefoot in the soil or on the beach. Although the shoreline isn't as solid as earth inland, there are other fantastic energies your body absorbs from a walk on the beach.

ACKNOWLEDGMENT

Now that you're grounded, you are ready to have your first communication with an animal. In my beginner workshops, I have participants bring photos of an animal they would like to work with in sessions. If you're ready to start, and you're with one of your animal friends, then the next step is acknowledging the animal.

Humans have many rituals around acknowledging other humans. When you talk with someone for the first time, ground rules need to be established so that each party understands how to keep themselves safe and operating within acceptable norms. One habit that humans engage in is mental defensiveness. If feeling a bit insecure, we manage our interactions with defenses such as judgment, "That's a ridiculous tie he's wearing," or we criticize ourselves, "I should have had a manicure this week. My hands are a wreck." When animals meet, they quickly establish territory issues, safety issues, and then go about getting to know one another in a wholehearted manner. Dogs sniff butts. Horses lean into their newly met friend horse to get the latest picture stories of its journey. Cats even enjoy the company of other animals. You can observe this when you see a few cats lounging around comfortably but not passed out asleep. They're probably sharing interesting information about their lives and even enjoying lively conversations.

Once you have established that you're safe in the company of an animal, that you're grounded and feeling relaxed in your own body, the next step is to open your heart and acknowledge what it is about the animal that you really like. The acknowledgement does not come from what you're thinking about; it comes from the pleasure of just being with another. You'll find that your heart opens naturally to the warmth you are sharing.

When I'm with an animal client, I give that animal my undivided attention and let it know that I'm a friend and that I'm listening. To be fully present with an animal is the strongest acknowledgement. They know that you're paying attention. And in my sessions with them, they also know a good deal about the issues that their human caregivers are seeking to understand.

I recently communicated with a fifteen-year-old shepherd mix that had stopped eating but had no outstanding health issues (according to his vet). He was eager to communicate; he told me he was through with living. When I dug a bit deeper, I found that his stomach hurt and that he was nauseated a lot. His human companion confirmed that he was on various drugs to control arthritis pain. I told her that her dog had lost his will to go on with life because of the constant stomach pain and nausea, all caused by the drugs! I suggested that she talk with her vet about alternative treatments, and I gave her a few suggestions that have helped other animals in my practice. She took the advice and called later to say that the vet had changed the prescriptions and that her dog was eating again.

In my workshops, I demonstrate acknowledgement by asking if anyone wants to be acknowledged. I always get plenty of eager hands in the air. I bring that brave student in front of the group and then proceed to say the things that automatically come from my heart. At this point, I'm so happy to see them and thankful that they came to take the course that it's easy for me to express my openness to their specialness. I may acknowledge that they have a wonderful smile or that I noticed how welcoming they had been to the other strangers around them. Sometimes I'll acknowledge their personal style and flair that brings cheer to the room. The words will come once you get over yourself and welcome the other with an open heart. Everyone loves this exercise.

I then ask if someone in the group wants to come forward and acknowledge me. This exercise is a bit more daunting. At this moment, I am aware that our human tendency to fear speaking in front of a group is usually stronger than our fear of death. When a brave soul comes forward to acknowledge me, I feel a profound sense of gratitude for the gesture. It is not easy to get up in front of strangers and open one's heart. That gesture exposes one's vulnerabilities and requires a great deal of trust. I appreciate the trust shown at that time. I'm grateful for them. Animals feel that same gratitude for us when we reach out and acknowledge them. Acknowledgement is the foundation upon which we build a community with our animal friends because it communicates vulnerability and trust.

One of my favorite clients is a retired movie star! His name is Deuk, and he is the beautiful black Friesian who was ridden by Antonio Banderas in the movie *Zorro*. After his successful stint as a Hollywood actor, he landed a dream job working with Kristi Ullman, who became his human guardian. Among their many athletic pursuits together, they have enjoyed years of dressage work, parades, and Roman riding just to mention a few. Kristi first called me years ago about a training issue. When it came to acknowledging Deuk, I was knocked off my feet! His heart is so big I felt like I was getting an enormous horse hug from him.

Kristi and I were on the phone, and she lives about three thousand miles from me in California. And yet I felt her friend's immediate ability to be present and fully engaged from the first instant. Animals like Deuk are evolved souls and have spent many lifetimes in positive relationships with humans. Their ability to trust and communicate makes working with them a joy. Deuk is pretty much retired now and keeps in touch. For the past few years, he has delighted his Facebook followers with his close kinship with a tarantula named Harry. Horses have wonderful friendships with their barn companions.

As humans, we each have our prejudices, phobias, and tastes. Humans are in the habit of casting inner fears upon our fellow creatures and responding to them with terror, disgust, or just plain dislike. (The opposite also holds true—we project our best onto certain animals.) I once had arachnophobia so severe that I spent one year training myself to overcome this fear.

The alligator I talked with can be an object of terror for some people. While they can be dangerous, they pose little threat to people who respect their boundaries. On Dewees Island, Hans and I kayaked into the territory of a twelve-foot bull alligator sunning on the banks of the little inland lake that had once been a duck hunting reserve. We were paddling within six feet of him when he gracefully slid into the water and then under our kayak, giving it a little bump. He meant no harm but was just letting us know whose territory we had entered. Never afraid, I felt instead a respect for this gesture and even a bit of affection for the old boy. When I communicated with him, he let me know he was enjoying the gesture as a bit of fun. I totally got it! I had acknowledged him fearlessly, and he acknowledged me.

As with any communication, acknowledgement does not automatically guarantee acceptance. We once had a black bear stealing seeds from our bird feeders. One day I walked into my office in the middle of the afternoon to witness the fellow sitting on his haunches, one foot from my office's French doors, with the birdfeeder tipped up and all the seed falling into his huge mouth! He was a male; I could see that at a glance. I called the family in, and we all stood on the other side of the glass, entranced. I communicated with the bear, and he was not too interested in our presence. He was hungry and said the seed was delicious. He didn't run away because he understood we didn't intend to hurt him. Feeling a little underappreciated in this exchange, I gently tapped on the window to get a more definitive greeting from him.

He paused for a second, and in one powerful "acknowledging" gesture, blew seeds out of his nose, all of them hitting the window with little pings. Then he went back to devouring the birdseed. Concerned that he might destroy my expensive squirrel-proof feeder (it wasn't bear-proof), Hans went out the front door with a pan and a wooden spoon and created an impressive racket that sent Mr. Bear scampering back into the woods.

There are animals that have been abused or abandoned or worse, and these souls present a bigger challenge in acknowledgement. Often these animals have a difficult time trusting humans. Many of my clients adopt cats and dogs from shelters, so I have the privilege of learning a lot about how an abused, neglected, or abandoned animal comes to trust humans again. It's a beautiful, healing process for both the human guardian and the animal.

There are ways to get around an animal refusing to respond to communication. As an intuitive, I can sense the hesitations from these animals, and I acknowledge them for needing to put up a protective shield. Just being acknowledged for needing to not talk helps build their trust. I will talk with the animal's guardian about their animal friend's issues, and the animal will slowly let down defenses during this process. At that point, I can usually continue the session, having gained a measure of trust. If that doesn't work, then proceeding with an empathic scan of the animal's energy field often opens things up considerably. One of the first things I'm aware of when I have a session is how my animal client is feeling physically. I'll acknowledge an ache or pain, and that's usually a good opening to a conversation. Animals are stoic by design and terrific at hiding health issues from their humans. But once they know they can trust you, they can give valuable information on the state of their health and are eager to talk.

For instance, as I was writing this I had a session with a horse living in Colorado. He was lame and hurting, and yet the vet could find nothing. But it was clear to the horse's guardian that something was wrong. The horse was communicative, and I had no trouble finding the "ouchy" spots and telling his story. A mare had been placed in his pasture for a week. She had proceeded to beat him up one night and ran him into the side of the pasture's run-in shed. He had gone over backward and had a number of soft tissue bruises as well as a sore tailbone. The human in this story had worked with me in the past and had complete trust in my work, and as a result of this level of trust, her horse was trusting also, and his trust enabled me to read him thoroughly. The information I conveyed to my human client allowed her to get the proper care for her horse and, happily, he recovered fully.

Acknowledgement emerges from the ability to feel vulnerable and trusting. If you are trusting, animals sense this and will offer you their trust in return. The key to bridging the divide between the two of you is acknowledgement. Once you master the art of acknowledging animals with an open heart, you are ready to enjoy the pleasure of reaching out and communicating with an animal.

TALKING WITH THE ANIMALS: BEING THERE

Because animals live in the present, there's a big difference between how we experience time and how they experience it. We humans spend a lot of time thinking about the past or projecting ourselves into the future. We pay so much attention to what's going on inside of our heads, that it's easy for us to lose track of what's happening in the present moment. And because we are such good storytellers, we live in the stories we give to the adventures our minds are engaged in at any moment.

Animals are good storytellers, but they don't dwell in their stories like humans seem to enjoy doing. For instance, most herd animals on pasture spend most of their days in a state that is deeply meditative. They're not thinking of anything! As we humans move through our day, we entertain ourselves in our minds with all manner of storytelling. When something happens, we naturally give it meaning, and if that meaning leaves us feeling unsettled, we will dwell on the story and, in a way, leave our bodies. It's human nature to compare something that is going on right now to something that happened in the past and then project that story out into the future. Our busy minds keep us thoroughly entertained and distracted.

Animals love stories too. When an animal is feeling safe in her territory, she will pass the time with a companion, sharing information in story form. It's a pleasure for them. But humans often take their own stories very seriously. Combine that with the human habit of judging the other or oneself in the moment, and it's difficult to stay focused on the here and now. We all wrestle with our inner critic who keeps us on our toes. Our judgmental self will keep us from enjoying the warmth of another's company. How can we enjoy the presence of someone we judge to be deficient in some way? There is no end to the misery the mind can cause for us humans! These traits are human defense mechanisms that can limit our ability to be authentic and vulnerable in this world.

In my workshops, I have my students break into groups and discuss the habits that keep them from being present in the moment. I can say from years of experience, it's the habit of judging others or criticizing the self that yanks us out of the pleasure of being present in the moment and sharing with another being our authentic self. When we are thoroughly comfortable in our bodies and relatively free from obsessive thinking, the heart opens, and we can enjoy the world around us. Coming to a place where the heart opens to another in a way that brings pleasure and love into the encounter is an essential skill in learning to communicate with animals. To enter this place, the student must master the darker forces in the personality, to transmute that darkness into a creative, life-enhancing energy that fills the personality with light.

I'd like to share an embarrassing story about myself—a story that became one of the defining stories of my life. I heard it enough times from my father that the behavior it describes became a part of my character. When I was a youngster and wanted a pony (What little girl doesn't want a pony?) my father used to tell a little story about me as a joke; he'd say that if I were offered the choice between a stall with a pony in it and a stall full of pony poop, I'd take the stall with the pony poop because I would want to know what the pony under all that poop was like. That's an odd story to tell about a child, and I had an odd father in a way. But the story, and its theme, stayed with me. It's a story about curiosity, but it's also a story about a certain degree of foolishness. My father's assertion, the one that ran my life in a way, was that out of curiosity I would rather take a big risk over a sure deal. That's the story of a gambler, and my father had a large appetite for gambling. But as it happens, I've always disliked games of chance. My father was projecting *his* character onto *me*!

This is what humans tend to do; we fail to really see the other because often we're projecting our hidden selves onto them. That's what my father did with me. It takes a lot of self-discovery for the receiver of such projection, particularly someone who grew up with it, to get to their authentic self. It is a journey that takes the mind into the myriad recesses of the soul, possibly a journey to places of hurt and fear. This journey requires courage. It's a necessary journey because it requires unmasking and mastering any fear or self-doubt, and when you emerge, you are so much more powerful in your newly acquired ability to accept your own vulnerability.

Once you become fully present in the moment and acknowledge another with an open heart, the vulnerability you show is profoundly comforting, and a connection is made in that instant. Communication becomes pleasurable. It's in this state of awareness that all things are possible. Let's explore the different ways a human may interact with another species.

SAY MORE ABOUT THAT: DEVELOPING YOUR SKILLS

There are four basic modes of communication. These represent the foundation of how information flows between species. There are many other ways, but these four comprise the core and are common to most animals and people.

Auditory. You hear what the animal says. Their thoughts come to you in words you hear in your mind. You ask a dog what his favorite toy is and he tells you, "It's a round thing that makes a squeaky noise." You ask the cat what her favorite food is, and she says, "Tuna."

Visual. You perceive pictures of what the animal is communicating. For instance, you ask a lost cat to describe the area he is in, and you receive a picture of a white building with a dark roof. You ask a horse to show you his pasture, and you "see" the fence, the run-in shed, and the woods beyond.

Kinesthetic/Empathic. You feel in your body sensations of what the animal you're communicating with feels. The horse you're talking with has a sore area in his right hip, and you feel this sensation of soreness in your right hip. The cat is hungry, and you feel the hunger pangs.

Knowing. This is detailed information that pops into your head during a communication session with an animal. These "packets" of information are clear and often full of verifiable detail. When working with a lost dog, you may get detailed information about the dog's adventure that is not visual, auditory, or empathic. The knowledge arrives like the content of a news story you're reading. These communications are surprising because all of a sudden you "know" things in great detail and yet don't know how they arrived fully developed in your mind! I call this kind of experience "psychic email."

In my everyday life, I'll "know" something that comes to me out of the blue. For instance, recently I was in Costco shopping, strolling down an aisle looking for the olive oil, when I felt a physical shock to my body, almost as if someone had intentionally rammed into me with a shopping cart. Since there was no one nearby, I filed the experience and went on with my shopping. Twenty minutes later, while returning home, my car was rear-ended at a stoplight. I was not seriously hurt but realized that while in Costco I received a psychic email download of the event.

As another example, when I was a college student, I crashed a lecture about an archeological dig in Turkey. The professor showed a slide from a rock pictograph depicting vultures flying over headless little stick bodies scattered about on the ground. The professor said that all anyone knew was that the pictograph was about funeral rites but that no one understood what the bird images meant. In that moment, I knew with an odd certainty that the bodies of the deceased were laid out in the wild and offered up to the vultures as a sacred gesture. I said nothing at the time because I was a nineteen-year-old art student not even majoring in anthropology. It was thirty years later that I saw a documentary about the practice of sky burials, largely a Tibetan practice today but traced all the way to southern Turkey, and that I understood what I had experienced at that lecture so long ago.

Everybody has one of these talents whether they are aware of it or not. In my workshops, I ask students to share their strongest ability with the group. In one workshop, I had a lawyer tell me that he used his "knowing" ability during the voir dire process (selecting the jury). He told us that when he questioned a potential jurist, he always "knew" how they'd vote during jury deliberation. He said he was seldom wrong.

There are other ways of sensing information. Earlier I mentioned psychic email. There is also "psychic smelling." I have a strong ability to "smell" what my clients are smelling, a sense called clairolfaction. My favorite story about this sense occurred years ago when I received a call from a woman who complained that her elderly indoor cat had suddenly become frantic with efforts to escape her home. She was truly baffled by this odd new behavior. While talking with the cat, I became aware of a strong smell of cinnamon. I asked her cat about the strong smell and learned that the cat found it intolerable. I mentioned this to my human client, telling her that the cat was terribly upset by the smell of cinnamon.

After a bit of a shocked pause, the woman confessed that because of an accident in her youth, the olfactory nerves in her nose were dead. She could smell nothing in her home, and she didn't want her visitors to smell cat litter. To solve the problem, she had placed cinnamon-scented plugins all around her home to mask any unpleasant smells! I suggested she remove them at once and keep the kitty litter clean then she need not worry about those smells. At the end of this session, my kitty client was happy. This is a reminder to use unscented litter because cats hate strong chemical smells!

There is another psychic ability that seems to go hand in glove with clairolfaction and that is clairgustance. This is the ability to taste something through psychic ability. I communicated with a cat that loved her human person and liked to sit on his lap. While we were talking I started to taste "sweet." I asked the cat about this taste, and she showed me that it was coming from the lap area of her friend. My client, the wife, confirmed her husband suffered from diabetes. I was "tasting" the sweetness that came from the sweet secretions on the diabetic's skin. The cat told me she sat on her person's stomach region to give "healing" power to his pancreas. Often I will ask a cat client what their favorite food is and I'll taste tuna!

BEGINNER'S EXERCISES

A big part of the animal communication learning process is own-ing your own intuitive sensitivities and sharing your experiences with trusted others. Do this often enough, and soon you accept how common psychic abilities are in the human experience. It's all about trusting your instrument.

Practice builds confidence. Here's a terrific beginner's exercise: With a friend, imagine the three primary colors—red, blue, and yellow. Let's say your friend goes first. As the sender, your friend might imagine a red fire engine, the blue sky, a yellow sunflower, or just disks of color. How you bring the color up in your mind is not as important as the image's color. So often I use a simple object like a red car when I do this exercise with a partner. As the receiver, your job is to center yourself, acknowledge your partner, and be present to any information that comes to you. You may see a bright red apple, taste lemonade, or remember the time you stretched out on the grass and stared up into the sky on a warm summer afternoon. You may hear the word: red.

Once you have an image clearly established in your head, share what you are seeing with your partner. Your partner then reveals the color they were trying to send. Again, it's best to keep with the primary colors for this first exercise. The simplicity helps build confidence.

Once you and your partner are getting it right almost every time, you can practice using simple shapes: circle, triangle, and square. The sender can get creative sending an image of a pizza slice for triangle, the image of the Moon for circle, or the image of a box for square. Also, you can project a story about one of the shapes to see what your partner picks up (knowing or psychic email)…something like, "I loved playing the triangle in the high school band." Creativity is at the heart of animal communication. At its foundation is the act of creation in the moment. The input you receive requires some assembly! You're creating a connection with someone else that is thoroughly unique. Learning animal communication should be fun.

THE INNER CRITIC

Usually at this point, everyone who's taken my course comes up against their inner critic, that voice that says, "You're not doing it right!" I remind students to thank that voice for sharing and tell them there is not a right or wrong way. There's just the way that the practice comes to each and every person, and it's always different.

One of the most gifted students ever to grace any of my workshops was a terrific woman who ran the largest no-kill animal shelter in her state. She did this while running her own manufacturing company! She was a human dynamo. She showed up so eager to learn that she was at my door a day early! I had to laugh I was so touched by her enthusiasm. It was clear after we began to practice that she had an enormous inner critic. During the seminar, she could not get a thing from her practice partners. She kept crying, "But I'm trying!!!" I told her to stop trying and just intend to get it. I assured her that it would come, to have patience.

When I begin each workshop, I tell the class that I've never had anyone fail to communicate with an animal. The criteria for success is getting information you could not have known from an animal you have just been introduced to by your partner. I go on to say that if one of them needs to be the first to fail, I will support them in that effort too.

This puts a bit of pressure on everyone. But it seems to work. My student was in tears by day two, having failed at every one of her attempts to communicate. I kept telling her that all was okay, that I supported her frustration and sense of failure. I would never judge her, and I believed in her. The pressure was immense for her as we entered our final session of the workshop on day two. I could hear her silently weeping in frustration as she struggled with her "you can't do this" critical self. It wasn't until the final fifteen minutes of the last session when I heard a shout of joy coming from her direction! She had made the breakthrough! A clear communication had come through to her, and her partner confirmed her accuracy. Tears of joy sprang from her eyes, and we all got chills hearing her share the story of her hard-won success. She went on to use her powerful gift in her work with her rescue animals. Remember her story after you hear that voice tell you "you can't do this." Getting past that inner critic is key to enjoying success.

DIALOGUE

At the moment my student from the story above finally had success, she told me she felt a strong rush of heartfelt energy. When your heart opens wide, there can be an exhilarating sensation, often accompanied by chills and a feeling of joy. We communicate with animals through our hearts; it's as simple as that. When you open your heart to another unconditionally, this powerful connection enables clear and authentic communication.

Deepening that communication involves the art of dialogue. Dialogue occurs when two beings share information and respond with interest and encouragement to each bit of information. For instance: Two people are discussing an event they both attended. Person one states that she liked the food at a restaurant. Person two asks what she liked in particular about the food. Person one then begins to share information on a deeper level. Compare this to an unsuccessful conversation: Person one states that she liked the food. Person two responds, "It was horrible." End of conversation! That is an example of a failed connection. Person one wanted to reach out with their information, but person two became trapped inside his own story with a strong judgment. This person could have opened up his heart, processed his "disgust," and at the same time exercised curiosity for the sake of dialogue. He might have learned something. The conversation might have led to rich discoveries for both participants.

Dialogue is the art of opening up a conversation to a deeper level. In animal communication, dialogue helps establish trust as the animal begins to appreciate that its concerns are being heard for what is often the first time! Many of my clients will laugh during a phone consultation and say that their animal seems to be hanging onto every word.

During a consultation, there are many opportunities to open a rich dialogue. A conversation might deepen out of the blue when an animal sends me a message (either in the form of a thought, an image, or a feeling), and I'll ask them to tell me more about it. A recent client (I'll call her Mary) lived with a cat (I'll call him Henry), who was not using the litter box for his daily pooh. The conversation started with me receiving a clear and strong image of another cat, a grey tabby—I reported this image and asked Mary who I was "seeing." She replied that she worked as a pet sitter and had many cats she took care of during the course of the week, and the cat I was seeing was a male cat in her care. I asked Henry what he thought of that and was told in plain language that he considered himself to be Mary's "cat husband" and that he didn't appreciate her spending time with another tomcat! From there we addressed his jealousy issue, which upon further conversation, we learned stemmed from an abandonment issue. During the session, Mary reported how relaxed Henry had become since we started the conversation. She told me that for the first time Henry, who had a bad habit of knocking the phone out of her hand while she was talking on it (jealousy), had been well-behaved!

To prepare possible dialogue for a communication with your animal, write down a set of questions you'd like to have the animal answer. As you'll see later on, for lost animals I prepare a specific set of questions such as:

Where were you when your current journey began?

In which direction did you travel?

Are there other people around you can show me?

For a more usual consultation, find out what your human client needs from the consultation and go from there. During the session, describe what you sense from the animal client to her human companion—her personality, spirit, anything that stands out. This will help everyone become more connected and frame the rest of the dialogue. The important thing as a beginner is to prepare some questions appropriate for the communication session. You will get answers. You may not get complete downloads, but you will get clues. And in the process of dialogue, a story will emerge.

During my first attempt at communication in a four-hour workshop I took in 1997, I talked with a sorrel thoroughbred mare. While I was working my way down a hastily assembled dialogue checklist, I empathically felt a "gassy" stomach, and I even burped! I asked the horse if she suffered indigestion, and she said yes. When I checked this out with my partner, she was able to confirm that the mare suffered from digestive issues. All she had provided me with was a photo of the mare as well as the mare's name, age, and breed. I've always been empathic, and to this day, that remains one of my core strengths. With practice, you will begin to appreciate your core strengths.

The next day, I was visiting a friend and sitting in the living room with her seven-year-old daughter. The girl had a sweet little female grey tabby on her lap. The daughter said she heard I could talk to animals, and I said I thought I could because I had just taken a class to learn how to communicate with them. She asked if I'd talk to her kitty, and I said yes. I introduced myself to the cat, admired her for a second, and asked if there was anything in particular she wanted her friend to know. The kitty promptly replied that she had a friend that visited her and then she showed me the image of an orange tabby climbing over the privacy fence of their backyard and trotting over to the sliding glass windows to say hi. I then thanked the cat for sharing and reported this information to my friend's daughter. Her eyes got very wide! "Yes," she said, "that orange tabby visits every day!"

The information shared with me during these two early communication attempts came because the mare and the cat both appreciated that I had a sincere interest in having a dialogue with them.

PRACTICING ON YOUR OWN: IT'S ALL YOUR IMAGINATION!

Once you've found your own natal skills in non-verbal communication, practice with as many animal friends as possible. I loved the excitement we shared as I had my first official animal communication session outside of the workshop confirmed. It was a moment of sheer joy and amazement.

The child I spoke with that day shared this moment with equal delight. Children talk with animals naturally, but by the age of seven or eight have been trained out of this native ability. It is common for children to have invisible friends. I've come to know that these invisible friends are real—they are usually young children who are in spirit visiting the living child. A young child can find great comfort and companionship from these relationships. Children appreciate and accept that there are other dimensions in this world and that other beings inhabit those dimensions. If you'd care to read more about communication with other realms, read *Proof of Heaven*[3] by Dr. Eben Alexander, a neurosurgeon and neuroscientist. In 2008 Dr. Alexander contracted bacterial meningitis and spent a week in a coma. The book is about his journey to a higher spiritual dimension and the life-altering experiences he had. It's about communication beyond the use of words and language and offers a scientific take on the phenomena.

Written and spoken language limits our thinking and communication to the rules built into its function. Living our lives as efficiently as possible comes about through language. Our entire day is structured towards thinking about what comes next and trying to clean up what just happened. We all experience running familiar "tapes" during the course of the day designed to facilitate just getting up and getting through the next twenty-four hours. Our minds become habituated to rationality and we lose the ability to engage in more creative, intuitive thinking. Artists and other creative people get specialized training in order to perceive the world in fresh and creative ways, but I've found that everyone benefits when stepping off the cow path and perceiving the world anew.

I've personally found that meditation and practicing mindfulness help to calm the chatter in my brain. Once calmed, I am able to notice more subtle forms of information in the environment. In my current state, I find myself practicing mindfulness almost automatically. To be an animal communicator, I need to be present in the moment. What happened yesterday or what might happen tomorrow have little power over me these days. In spite of this, I have a terrific memory. To this day, I can recall vivid details of communications I had with animals many years ago.

I live on Warrior Mountain in the Blue Ridge Mountains of North Carolina. I've lived here for many years and have grown close to the wild animals that share territory with me. Last summer I was in the kitchen when I heard what I've come to recognize as warning cries from the large cardinal population that nests in our azalea bushes each summer. I have a strong heart bond with these birds as they're my now deceased mother's totem animal and always bring news of her presence. On any given day, there will be alarm cries from the flock as there are many predators prowling the forest floor. On this day, the alarm cries were exceptional and even I became alarmed. I felt in my heart the anguish these birds were communicating. When I stepped outside of my kitchen, I could see at least five of the bright red males on the driveway, hopping about and crying shrilly. I walked over to the scene and saw curled on the surface of the driveway a large black snake with twelve distinct egg-shaped bulges in his long body. The snake had just robbed a number of nests in the azalea bushes and was so stuffed he could not move.

I walked right up to where he lay curled up in a stupor. I knew this black snake well. He had chased off the swallows that had begun to nest in the eaves of our carport—they simply gave up making their nests there after repeated raids by this fellow. We've seen him climb up the side of our house many times in an attempt to get at the Carolina wren nest in the flower baskets hanging from our eaves. My heart went out to the cardinal family. The black snake is also my friend. He eats many rodents that plague my garden, and he is friendly in his own way. This has been his territory for a long time, and he appreciates that we live with him in harmony.

Accepting nature as it is takes wisdom. Animals respect the cycle of life—of birth and death. It is our job to also come to terms with this cycle. Being at peace with the cycles of life and death brings the wisdom that supports clear communication. To bring in judgment is to block the flow of information. Judgment should come after you've gathered all of the facts and should be used to help shape your world to make better sense of it. If you are judging the natural world from a point of view that makes others "bad" because of their natural impulses, then your world is going to feel a bit off tilt.

Animals do not share the values of humans. Animals need to be accepted and respected on their own terms. Their acceptance of domestication signals their willingness to share our environment. It is up to us to work with them to facilitate this process. So I acknowledged the grief and anger of the cardinals, and the prowess and greed of the snake and left well enough alone. The birds eventually went about their business and returned to their normal routines, and the snake, after a long while, slithered away into his own world, probably sated for a long time to come.

It is important to remember that the body is the instrument for receiving these extra-rational communications. By learning to trust one's intuition, honor the imagination, and suspend judgment, the skills needed to communicate with animals can be regained and refined.

Confidence comes with practice.

THE PRACTICE

*H*aving learned and practiced the fundamentals of animal communication, you are ready to begin helping others with your newfound skill. But before you dive in professionally, I'd like to acquaint you with what I think are some essential considerations in dealing with your human and non-human clients, the kinds of challenges and situations you will likely encounter, and some approaches I've used in dealing with them.

THE TWELVE CORE NEEDS OF ANIMALS

Human relations specialists in most major organizations have likely been trained in Maslow's Hierarchy of Needs, which is basically a theory, represented in pyramid form, of human needs from the very basic (at the bottom of the pyramid) to the more refined (top of the pyramid). The point of the theory is that organizations ignore these needs at their peril, and organizations considered to be more mature are those that successfully meet their employees' needs from the base of the pyramid to as near the top as possible.

With that in mind, it's essential to remember that in any animal communication session you have *two* clients, and you are most likely having the session with them because the needs of one or the other—or both—are not being met, at least not completely. Being human, I'm going to assume that you are reasonably familiar with what makes us do the things we do. But what about animals? What makes them tick?

During my early years communicating with animals, I also studied astrology. I quickly realized that astrology was a well-established discipline that I could tweak and leverage to help me understand what might be going on in the lives of my clients in my animal communication practice. I've been using my knowledge of astrology to support my practice with animals for the last twenty years.

An astrological chart cast for a communication session can provide concise information on issues that might come up during the session. The chart can also reveal a lot about the animal's nature as well as that of the human on the other end of the phone. I'll detail the specifics of using astrology in animal communication later, in a section devoted just to the subject. You can certainly skip that section if you are not interested. For now, though, I want to share the exciting linkages I've applied from the art of astrology to my communication practice.

An astrological chart is composed of a round circle divided into twelve pie-shaped sections. Each of the twelve sections is called a "House," and each House of a completed chart has a planetary ruler that relates to a set of needs. Additionally, when the chart is cast, each House falls in general alignment with one, and sometimes across two, astrological signs. You've probably heard of these signs—zodiac signs such as Aries or Pisces or Capricorn. The exact configuration of any astrological chart is specific to the date, time, and place for which the chart is cast. In my work, the Moon's House, her sign, and the connections she makes are very important. As the great astrologer Noel Tyl taught me: the Moon represents "the reigning need" of the personality.[4] The Houses of the chart represent the area of life in which the need is expressed. The astrological sign represents the nature of the Moon's expression through the sign. For instance, a Moon in Leo, according to Noel, often will have "a King Complex"—a need to be the center of attention.

I noticed that by casting a consultation chart, that is, an astrological chart for the exact time and date of the planned consultation with my clients, I could pair my animal client with one of these needs pretty quickly by using the position of the Moon and the House it occupies! You don't have to have the animal's birth information for this to work. What you will pick up is the core need being expressed for the purpose of the communication. I've rarely had this system fail me. Here's my list:

1. Need to be number one. This animal is a natural athlete and loves to compete. This is your boss mare or your little dog that is demanding that he get fed first. This animal expresses Moon in Aries energy. He's a leader.

2. Need to establish security and keep things the same and beautiful. This is your bomb-proof horse, stubborn dog, or lazy cat. It is the dog that follows the same routine daily or the cat that loves nothing more than the pleasure of lying in the Sun. These animals can be creative, stubborn, unfazed by drama, and are often beautiful. Sometimes in seminars I have students ask an animal to give them a poem, and these animals deliver some amazing poems! These are the Moon in Taurus creatures.

3. Need to have a lot of variety. These are the forever-curious animals, the seekers. I do a lot of lost animal work looking for these characters. They are forever wandering off on a "checking out the neighborhood" adventure. They want variety and need a lot of stimulating activity. They love agility, short trips, puzzles, and learning new things. This is your dog that notices every squirrel on the block while out on a walk. This is the cat that has to be rescued from between the floors of the house because she

found that one little spot to squeeze through so she could explore the world between the floors. These are the Moon in Gemini animals.

4. Need to be emotionally available, to feel secure, and to experience belonging. This is the nanny dog that cares about everyone. This is the kitty that snuggles with you when she senses your sadness. This is the pony that opens his heart to every child that hugs his neck. These are the caretakers of the world. This is the expression of a Moon in Cancer.

5. Need to give love, to shine for others, and to be the center of attention. This is the show horse that's so beautiful and talented that all eyes are on her. This is the little goat out in the pasture whose antics have all eyes on him. These animals are natural performers and tend to have a bit of a king or queen complex and are prone to be natural actors always "hamming" it up. This is the Leo Moon expression.

6. Need to do things exactly right, to be correct, to be insightful. This is the fussy cat that will eat only on a clean dish on a pristine surface. She'll groom herself until every hair is in place. This is the dressage horse that can master advanced movements with grace and ease but may have a nervous breakdown if he can't be perfect. This is your dog that likes to pick up all her toys and have them in one spot, just so. This Moon is in Virgo.

7. Need to be appreciated and popular. These are the pleasers. They can become nervous around disagreements and will more quickly act to resolve them. There's a wonderful video circulating on Facebook that shows two golden retrievers nose to nose, each holding one end of a toy. The look on their faces is

intense as the fight for control ensues. A third retriever enters the scene and calmly places her nose on top of and between the noses of the two combatants, breaking the stalemate. She's your Libra Moon dog. These are the animals that will do anything to please and foster cooperation and peace.

8. Need to be in control, deep, self-sufficient, and right. Sometimes aloof, always intense, these animals are good at establishing trust in relationships. They demand integrity and will get controlling if relationships are out of balance. Once trust is established, they'll support you always. This is the dog that has your back. This is the cat that can change the energy of your home for the better. This is the horse you can trust with your life. Fearless, deep, with a well of healing energy, these are the animals that are silently putting things right in the unseen world around us. They are often shamans and healers. These are the Scorpio Moon animals.

9. Need to have one's opinion respected. These animals are good at figuring things out, of putting information together in such a way that they understand underlying principles and philosophies. Often brilliant, curious, and generous, they can also be strongly opinionated. These are the sheriffs who know what the rules and regulations are and will try to enforce them. This is the dog that will tell on another dog that's done something wrong. Enthusiasm is a big part of the personality. They'll be the first to greet you when you return home. These are the Sagittarius Moon animals.

10. Need to make things happen. These animals are ambitious and good at strategizing and planning for

a goal. This is the competitive horse in the Hunter class who takes his jumps seriously and plans ahead to make sure he gets the best score he can manage. This is the dog that knows mealtime is coming and rounds up his people and any other dogs at the precise hour to make sure they're in the kitchen getting the food in their bowl. These are the CEOs of the animal world. They are in charge of getting things done. These are the Capricorn Moon animals.

11. Need to do their own thing, the maverick or rebel. These animals are often aloof and enjoy a variety of communities. They like to be helpful and will come to the aid of anyone in a crisis. They often love to be loved but sometimes don't know how to give love back. This is the cat that will leave home if she gets bored or decides she doesn't like you. This is the dog that seems a bit peculiar but gets along with everyone. This is the horse that counts among his friends a spider, a cat, a goat, and a herd of deer. These are the Aquarius Moon animals.

12. Need to be sensitive, idealistic, and impressionable. This is the animal that lives sometimes in another dimension. This dog always seems to be staring off into space but with a little grin on her face. This is the cat that seems to drift about the house in a fog, responding to unseen "friends." This is the horse that stands in the pasture for hours dreamily looking into the woods. These are our animal poets, artists, and space cadets. They can be wonderfully sweet. Above all, they are masters of dreaming. These are the Pisces Moon animals.

Each animal has a dominant need, and when you pay close attention to that need, a pattern becomes clear. At present, we have three cats in our household. Maisie, going on three years, is a dilute calico shorthair with strong healing energies. Her eyes bore right through you. She's always looking deep into matters. She needs to be important, deep, intense, and is easily offended when ignored. Her trust is fierce, and when she doesn't like something, she'll let you know. She needs to know where she and you stand. She's an obvious Scorpio Moon.

Major Tom, also going on three years, is a mellow little orange and white space cadet domestic shorthair with an adorable overbite. He's a dreamer and quite happy sitting by himself for hours staring into space. I know he's entertaining a wonderful inner world during these periods. He's calming to be around. He's a sweet Pisces Moon cat.

Mr. Big is a nine-year-old Ragdoll we recently adopted. He's quite serious and in command. Although not pushy, he is right there if anything should go amiss. When Tommy gets too rough with Maisie, he'll rush over and break things up. He's a bit of a sheriff and a bit of a CEO and a bit of a Libra. We recently had to evacuate due to a storm, and he was very helpful with the younger cats, getting them calmed down with his soothing presence. He has a sweet side too and will purr softly when held. With his calm, in-command personality, I'd say he's a Capricorn Moon cat.

Each animal has many selves inside just like humans. There's the hunter, the lover, the beach bum, the princess, and many more. It's fun to observe these aspects in the animals I work with. The strongest example of the need to shine for others and be admired and the center of attention is Deuk, the Friesian I mentioned earlier. He is supremely aware of himself as a beautiful, talented, and expressive personality. He delights in the rituals of being a show animal. He loves being adored, and he also adores his person, Kristi. He has a king complex! I would say he's a Leo Moon horse.

Everyone knows the animal that needs to be number one! He's the dog at the head of the pack, getting fed first, always out in front demanding to be the leader. He doesn't cooperate well and will nose right past you if your needs don't suit his. I have a neighbor with a beautiful Carolina dog. I've never been able to make friends with her because she isn't interested in anything outside of her territory, which she absolutely dominates. She's an Aries animal and barely has the time of day for me!

On the other side of our house is a sweet Great Dane that seems to be the type that just wants to keep things the same, pleasant, and stable. When our neighbors first moved in, she seemed frantic with anxiety and clearly didn't like being uprooted. However, once she settled into a fixed routine, she was great, and life became very pleasant again for her. I think of her as our Taurus neighbor: Happy with the routine pleasures of life.

A NOT SO TYPICAL COMMUNICATION SESSION: WHAT TO EXPECT WHEN YOU BEGIN

I say this because no session you'll encounter could be labeled "typical." All sessions will yield surprises and rewards and maybe even disappointment. It's all to be expected.

A recent client who called from a state out west is a perfect example of the kinds of things you can run into. I'm changing names and not using the state's name to protect the deer herd in this story, which could become easy targets for unethical hunters.

My human client, Linda, wanted to visit with her five-year-old mule deer buck named George and her two-and-a-half-year-old Georgian Grande dressage horse in training named Henry. I was looking forward to the conversations because I had recently been introduced to the relatively new Georgian Grande breed and found them to be very articulate and good conversationalists to boot. As an added bonus, this was my first communication with a wild deer that had befriended a human.

I first visited the young Georgian Grande colt, Henry. He told me training was going well, that he had a good sense of humor, and that he was a bit of a clown—all confirmed by Linda. Although he was gelded, I could tell he was a bit "studdish," and she confirmed he was indeed an alpha horse. He showed me the precision of his movement, his stylish collection, and verticality, all of which made him very proud. He said he knew about dressage from his barn mate who was proficient in the sport, and he loved its creativity. Although he hadn't yet been ridden, that would come at age four, Linda was getting him ready.

Henry, a gorgeous blue roan, had been paying attention to all the other horses at the barn and knew that dressage was a beautiful sport, and he communicated to me dressage was what he had his heart set on mastering. However, Linda said that later in his training she would introduce him to other disciplines such as jumping to give him a choice. Like any youngster, he was already dreaming of being an accomplished adult.

Horses are very talkative amongst themselves in a barn like the one in which Henry lives. He also spends much of his time in the pasture with other horses, so he's very happy with his life. At his barn, there's an indoor dressage arena, and he knows from the other horses what goes on there, what's important, what pleases the humans, and what the horses themselves enjoy. At this point in the conversation, another horse came into focus—Judy, a sixteen-year-old bay mare that is Linda's current dressage horse. She piped in to express her jealousy of the young colt Linda was spending so much time with. Judy's stall was across the barn's aisle, and she lived in another pasture. But she knew the score! Linda told me that Judy was hot and impatient—she was all business, just wanting to get the job done. She was also possessive, self-assured, and a bit vain! She enjoys the show ring and has great self-esteem.

Then I heard someone say, "I'm a champion" and assumed it was Judy. Linda said no, that was her retired twenty-seven-year-old roping horse, Bill—he was the champion. Since Bill is also a bay, I had not caught the switch in the conversation—I was still talking with a bay-colored horse. When I'm talking with someone with more than one animal, this cross talk is common, and it can lead to a bit of confusion. Most animals during a session pay close attention to what their human is saying, and in this case, Linda was on her toes helping me keep her horses straight. Bill had been a roping champion, and in Linda's words, was smart and level-headed. He is a foundation quarter horse, built solid and with a solid personality. His retirement job is living on pasture with his friend Judy and a small group of young horses. Bill told me that he entertains the youngsters and tells them of his exploits and that they all admire and look up to him. Judy said her job is just to teach them manners and to respect mares!

One thing Linda wanted me to talk with Judy about was a big door on a sidewall of the arena used to bring the tractor in and out of the facility. Linda told me Judy doesn't like the door and neither do a lot of the horses in the barn. I took a long look at the door and saw the image of a very big snake over the door. I checked with Judy who said the dangerous snake was guarding the door and that the horses all saw this image. I shared her concerns with Linda who said that there had been a problem with snakes coming in under the door. Horses are very sensitive to what goes on in a barn. One of the barn's dogs had a close call with the snake. All of the horses were talking among themselves about this snake and had blown the size of the snake to the size of the door! I did a little energy work (see the section on energy cleansing) to clear the arena and suggested they perform a ritual and lay down some type of snake repellant in a semi-circle around the outside of the door, from frame to frame.

Next in the consultation, I visited with the magnificent five-point buck, George. George showed himself emerging from the woods next to a brown structure. Linda told me I was seeing her neighbor's house and that was indeed where he often emerges. Next he told me that he has a family of five does. He showed them to me. There was a slight pause and then Linda said in amazement, "Yes! He has a family of five does, and I've given each of them a name!" I was as surprised as she was. Linda had been invited to be part of a family of deer. That was a first for me, and I felt honored to be introduced to Linda and her deer family.

George had broken his leg the year before, and Linda had fed him and protected him until it mended. She wanted to know how he broke his leg and how he mended it. He showed me that he was running, and he sailed off a rock. When he came down, his leg ended up wedged between two rocks and snapped. He said he willed it to heal and it did. Linda said that was true, that when he showed up at the house, it was broken and protruding from the skin. (She sent photos, and the injury would have destroyed most deer.) She said he was now running on it. Linda also said that if a deer injures a leg, the corresponding antlers will be stunted until the injury heals. Now, on George's right side, he does not have five points—he only has three in the usual arrangement and a fourth that sticks straight out in front, providing George with a formidable weapon.

George is Linda's spirit animal. He and his family, when it is not rutting season, spend afternoons on her lawn, enjoying themselves. Talking with George gave me chills as I connected with the power of the love and connection between human and deer.

I started the session as I always do by casting a consultation chart. In my practice, I use the Sixth House to represent my client's animal. I could tell from the chart I was going to enjoy the meeting. Jupiter, the planet that rules horses, was the chart's ruler, and Taurus was on the cusp of the House that represented the animals I would talk to. That clued me into the nature of her animals—beautiful, solid, stubborn, pleasure-loving creatures of Venus, the planet of love and harmony. Below is the consultation chart for this session. I'm putting it here so that those familiar with astrology can follow along. For everyone else, don't worry: I go into how to read these charts later in the book.

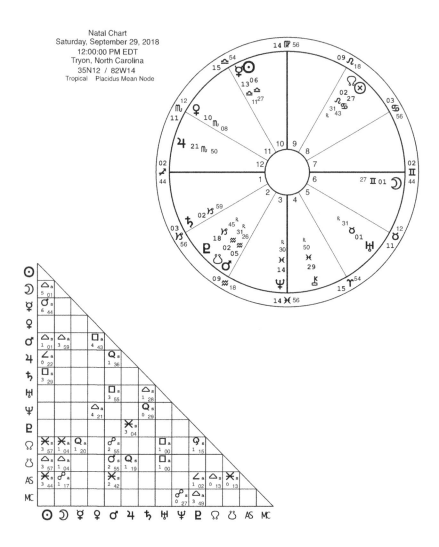

Figure 1 - Linda's Consultation Chart

In this chart, the Sun is in Libra, and the Moon is in Gemini, providing a lovely energy (Libra Sun) flowing into the need to be informed and to share thoughts and ideas. With Sagittarius rising, Jupiter in House Twelve, and Neptune opposing the Midheaven, there's a delightful spiritual element. Linda's relationship with George felt to me as if it were carrying a deep spiritual energy—a relationship that spanned the centuries. Linda felt the same way.

You'll also see in this chart that Taurus is on the cusp of the Sixth House, and since Venus rules Taurus, Venus becomes the ruler of the Sixth House. And, as you'll see later, for a consultation chart, the Sixth House becomes the Ascendant of the chart I use for human clients' animals. That means that Linda's animals are ruled by the planet Venus, which is in the sign of Scorpio.

I asked Linda if she would be willing to provide feedback on what this session meant to her. Here are her words:

The session was nothing short of profound for me, opening my heart to a world of intrigue while providing an immense amount of peace, appreciation, and thanks for the true blessings that I have been bestowed.

I visited the horses shortly after our session and experienced chills from head to toe when approaching each of them, knowing them now on a deeper level and identifying with their thoughts, concerns, and feelings. I now feel that I can provide them with sensitivity to each of their needs and be better for each of them in our future journeys together.

Regarding George, it is truly an unprecedented bond, I feel both honored and grateful for his presence, trust, and will. Deer are flight animals as are horses, bred to flee when danger is near. The sheer fact that he has allowed me into his world, finds refuge here, and trusted me when he was at his weakest is miraculous. I look forward to my future and the path it takes me with all of God's creatures, but I am extremely excited about how my relationships with my portion of the animal kingdom will continue to develop and evolve, and I will continue to give thanks for each of their spirits having so powerfully enriched my life.

My animal friends have changed my life; their presence has completed me. I am deeply humbled as I appreciate how all the animals in my life have helped put back together all of my lost pieces.

ABANDONMENT AND WORKING WITH LOST ANIMALS

I've heard that the first true scare a child experiences is often that moment right after they start to walk—when they walk away, turn around, and cannot see the parent who is guiding their steps. Toddlers can go ballistic in grocery stores if they totter away from mom and turn a corner and lose track of her. The emotion going through the child is the terror of abandonment. It can come in a number of experiences. Incidents caused by accidents, abuse, neglect, and most commonly just turning around and not seeing mom can leave psychic scars. As adults we've long lost the memory of such an event, but we retain the pain from the scar, and it can be triggered later in life. In my practice, I find that going through losing an animal can be an enormous trigger for abandonment issues.

As I mentioned earlier, I had a heartbreaking firsthand experience with this feeling before I became a communicator, when my Siberian husky, Sara, was stolen in the middle of the night. I woke up to her brother Cutter's howling outside and ran down to the dog run to find him standing alone, calling for his sister. I immediately felt sick to my stomach. Sara was gone, and my abandonment issue kicked in powerfully. I felt incapacitated.

The next morning I used the powerful emotions surging through my body to launch a search and rescue effort. I brought in two animal communicators, hired Sherlock Bones, and posted a large reward to help me find Sara. I spent hours calling vets, shelters, and neighbors. Weeks went by, during which time my family and I suffered the emotional rollercoaster of promising leads that turned out to be false alarms.

You'll recall that we eventually did find Sara. The ordeal took exactly one month from start to finish. The emotional impact, unbearable at first, propelled me to fight to find Sara, and from that fight, I developed a keen understanding of my own feelings of abandonment. I went from feeling like a victim to feeling victorious.

I work a lot with lost animals. There is an art to the practice, and not every communicator wants to take up that art. I became a communicator a year after Sara's ordeal and decided that I would take all lost animal calls out of gratitude for the two communicators who helped me with Sara. Developing the skill of working with lost animals required helping my human clients manage strong feelings of abandonment that arise during the crisis.

One of the biggest problems I encountered during my long learning process was not being able to discern if the animal was in or out of their body. If an animal dies suddenly, such as when being hit by a car or taken prey by a predator, it can be hard for them to know that they've suddenly transformed from embodied to spirit. It's just like in the movie *The Sixth Sense*. The character played by Bruce Willis doesn't know he's dead, and a mysterious young boy, played by Haley Joel Osment, helps him in his journey to discover his true condition. In the end, the boy guides him to accept the fact that he had been murdered the year before. As I've mentioned, sometimes animals take fantastic journeys when they're lost, sending back visual images of discernable landmarks. I tell my clients that if the animal does not know he's dead, I might not be able to tell. I do question the animals thoroughly to determine their fate. Often the animals will show me a close up of a predator's face or body as the last thing they remember.

A couple in Greenville, SC called in tears when they lost their beloved miniature poodle mix. The dog had escaped when a fence gate was left ajar. I tracked the dog through the neighborhood over the course of a few days. The method I use is called "remote viewing." I can actually "see" where the animal has traveled. I get specific landmarks, which are easy for my clients to identify and helps to keep spirits high. I kept assuring my clients that their dog was a capable adult and was taking care of himself. To them, he was their child, and so their feelings of abandonment were extremely painful. I encouraged them to use the golden cord technique—to imagine a golden cord going from their hearts to their dog's heart. When we do this exercise, we send energetic messages to our lost animals that we are keeping them in our hearts and making every effort to reunite with them. I have found that animals are very sensitive to how we feel during their absence and often interpret our feelings of distress as somehow their fault. The golden cord helps set up a positive energetic connection that supports both human and animal.

I saw that the little dog had finally settled into a shelter near a small factory with a loading dock. The dog had gotten the attention of people who worked on the dock, and they had begun to leave food out for him. I passed this information to my clients. The dog was safe, sheltered, and had found a food source. Many lost animals make this their priority. I have had many reunions near dumpsters behind fast-food restaurants. My clients were eventually able to locate this factory from the description the dog had given. And it was there, near the loading dock, that they were blissfully reunited. They reported back to me that, for the week their dog was missing, workers at the factory fed him.

The following is a story written by Elaine Keene of Nova Scotia describing her animal communication session with me when her cat Andre went missing, illustrating the frustrations and challenges of looking for a lost loved one:

> *In April of 2016, we had just moved into a newly built house. There was still a lot of work to be done (including a kitchen install that was delayed). Andre, our ten-year-old Ragdoll had always been an indoor cat, but he had been so unhappy in recent months, and the area that we had moved to was quiet and very cat friendly, so we felt it was in his best interests to finally be allowed outside. So we started allowing him out in late June.*
>
> *One early August evening, Andre went out. As usual, I waited up for him. Pretty much slept on the couch. When he*

didn't return home by morning, the family started looking for him. Walked the streets daily, calling for him. We called and visited the local SPCA, and we posted notices on Kijiji—a Canadian buy and sell website—and the local lost pet websites. On September 8, I finally contacted Diane about a session. We spoke later that day. She described how Andre was feeling and what he was seeing as he left—the local barn owl and the houses of families that he liked to visit because they gave him food. [She also] *told us that he was really unhappy with all the noise from the building and that he had not been feeling very loved for the past six months or more. All very understandable, as I was pretty much at my wit's end from managing the house build and the associated financial stress—lack of sleep and the recent loss of my mom as well as having a thirteen-year-old golden retriever with cancer that we were trying to battle through natural methods. Anyhow, Diane talked to him and told him that we were sorry, that we missed him, loved him, and would really like it if he would agree to come home. He was getting lots of love from frequenting a home with a child who paid him lots of attention, and he wasn't really convinced to come home but agreed to think about it. He felt that he probably knew his way home if he decided to do so. She sent out visualizations for him to find his way home and told us it might take a while for him to decide to come home and also some time for him to make his way home.*

Diane described the surroundings of where he was hanging out. I drove around the city for days and never did find a place that [fit the description].

She told me about the golden cord and taught me some visualization and intention exercises to connect me to Andre.

She also suggested the Sherlock Bones book to follow steps to try to find him. I bought it and ended up putting up about two hundred more posters offering a reward. I became more crazed and desperate as the days went on. I put up so many posters, that even after I thought I had taken them all down, I would be in an area and see one and not even remember putting it up!

On Sept 13, I sent her an email to let her know that he was still not home and to send her pictures of our house to help her visualize to help him find his way home.

Hi Diane,

Andre is still not home. You had mentioned that you would continue to visualize our reunion, so I thought I would attach pictures of our front and back yards in the hope that it will help to guide him.

I took your advice and bought the Sherlock Bones book. We have made a poster and distributed copies around all schools, supermarkets, and traffic choke points in the city. I can't saturate any particular area since I don't know where he is. I have located about 125 above ground pools in the city and have driven the streets and ensured posters are nearby.

In listening to the recording once again, I noticed that I never clearly stated how much I miss him and need him back in my life. My heart is truly aching for him; however, I am trying to now let go and let the universe bring him back to me if that is what is meant to be. I am using the golden cord technique, but I am so anxious about his leaving that it is hard to envision and project all the love he will come back to.

If he doesn't come back in another couple of weeks, I will consider scheduling another appointment.

To which she replied:

On 13/09/2016 11:42 AM, Diane Samsel wrote:

Dear Elaine,

Thank you for this update, and I'm so sorry that Andre is still missing. As I was typing this, I had a strong image of Andre at a cat colony in your area. This is often what happens when cats go missing; they find the colony where food is available. I would recommend that you locate (if you haven't already) the local group that supports the cat colonies.

Good luck with Sherlock Bones!

Warmly,

Diane

When I got her email, it was so off the wall and so completely different than the scenario that we had discussed earlier, with the small child and absent parents, I was incredulous. I was thinking—is she talking to the right client? Maybe she has me confused with someone else? All of a sudden, I was unsure about the whole procedure, and even though I'm a pretty strong believer, my faith was quite shaken. The next day, on Sept 14, my daughter got a call regarding the notice that she had posted on Kijiji. The woman said, "I think I have your cat. It looks like the picture you posted, and it's wearing a beaded collar." The woman just lived about six blocks away—still in our neighborhood. My daughter and I raced over—bracing ourselves for the possibility that it wasn't him as we had had a couple of false alarms over the month he had been missing.

We showed up at her house. She had him trapped in the garage with some litter and some food. It was him!! After thirty-four days we had our boy back! He was freaked out and didn't come to us—he just wanted to hide. It was so strange; I had assumed that he would come running to me as soon as he saw me. Anyhow, it was a tearful, joyous reunion. We thanked the lady and tried to give her the money that we had offered for the reward, but she declined it.

Then she told us that he had just shown up two days earlier, and she knew that there was a new cat around because one of her five cats was not very happy about yet another cat showing up and had been growling at him. She really didn't want to have to take another one in. It was a cat colony indeed!

Diane, I can't tell you how much I appreciate the work that you do and how grateful I am for the help you have given our family with both Andre and Corey.

Warmest regards,
Elaine

WHEN LOST ANIMALS GIVE GOOD INSTRUCTIONS

A good many of my lost animal cases are resolved in time. It can be difficult to live with the feeling of helplessness an owner experiences not knowing where their companion is and if their friend is being fed, sheltered, and protected. Years ago I received a call from a woman whose elderly indoor cat had vanished from their deck while the cat was sunbathing. She was feeling terrible for all the usual reasons, but the added burden of worrying about an elder with no experience outdoors made this case especially poignant.

I made contact with the cat who then described her journey. While on the deck, a wild animal—here she showed me what looked like a groundhog—lumbered by, frightening her. She dashed off the deck and ran for her life. Before she knew it, she was lost. She had come to rest in a field and described in detail where she was. A specific detail that ended up being important involved a pile of rocks in a field. She told me to tell her person that she was sheltered in those rocks. Later, my client wrote to tell me that she finally found her cat exactly where she said she'd be waiting for her, on the pile of rocks in a pasture, but it was a mile away! She said her cat had lost a lot of weight but was otherwise in good shape.

Another client, Kelly McGowan, called me one afternoon, deeply upset. She had arrived home to find her two-year-old domestic shorthair Russian Blue, Tank, run over in the road in front of her home. We talked over the course of a few days as it turned out Tank wanted to return to her with a new body. He gave me exact instructions that included an old barn a few miles down the road from her house. She was to turn right there and proceed to a farmhouse on the left where a "free kittens" sign was in the front yard. Kelly followed the instructions and found the farmhouse, the sign, and a box of six-week-old kittens! Among the kittens was a domestic shorthair Russian Blue that looked exactly like Tank. She adopted him, named him Tank, and over the years reported that the new kitten grew up to have the exact same personality. She sent photos of both cats, and they are identical looking as adults.

When I work with lost animals, the first thing I do is track them. I ask them to describe the landmarks they pass on their journey. I ask them to show me where the Sun rises and sets to determine the direction they're headed. Sometimes I "see" the orientation of their journey (whether north, south, east, or west). It's difficult for animals to judge distances, especially if the lost animal has been transported in a car. My dog Sara was about twenty-four miles from home when she was first contacted after she was stolen, and she wasn't able to give the communicator who reached her there a clear indication of her location.

As an animal communicator, you will likely run into a case in which the "lost animal" simply doesn't want to be found. As it happens, I had such a case recently, a "missing cat" case. In this case, the cat was staying inside the van parked at the hotel where a couple moving to a new state lodged for the evening. They had their household possessions in the van, and thieves stole the van in the middle of the night, taking the cat with it. The cat's name is Clyde, an eight-year-old domestic longhair Russian Blue mix.

I became acquainted with this case through a woman named Anne who lives in the area and contacted me to help in the search for Clyde. Anne is a scientist, who also happens to be a talented communicator, although she doesn't use her communication skills professionally. When I contacted Clyde, he showed me the area where he took refuge after escaping from the van when the thieves stopped for gas. He was very clear about buildings, landmarks, and topography. He showed me a house where he was getting food.

Anne was able to make contact with the family that was feeding Clyde. The housewife had taken a photo of the cat the family was feeding, and it looked like a skinny version of Clyde (he'd been gone for a few weeks at that point). The cat in the photo appeared to be the same size, have the Russian Blue coloring, long hair, the same long fluffy tail, and the same close-set yellow eyes. Clyde had described to me a striped, shorthaired, orange cat that had become his friend, and the family feeding him had an orange tabby family member that fit that description. Clyde told me he was staying near or under an outbuilding on the property. He also told me he was enjoying being an outdoor cat.

Attempts were made then to recover Clyde, but unfortunately, he didn't respond to the rescue efforts. No one could catch him. He was communicating that he liked being free too much. Since there was food; safe places to hide; and best of all, plenty of hunting, he wanted to stay free. He vanished from the house where he had been sighted and photographed.

Since then, Anne and I kept in touch with Clyde and followed his adventures. He had taken up residence in a concrete structure like a culvert. There were other cats in the territory who were his friends. This little colony was getting food from a home in the same neighborhood that was feeding several strays. Anne was able to track down the house and show the occupants a photo of Clyde. They confirmed that he was one of the strays they were feeding. This house was on the edge of the neighborhood he was hanging out in. There was a slope behind the houses that led down to the gas station where Clyde had made his escape weeks prior. He was getting to know the territory. However, he stopped being seen at this feeding station and seemed to vanish.

Later, Anne contacted me again, and I checked in with Clyde. He showed me that he was hiding in a dark place, and there was a big metal pole in his field of vision. He let me know he had left the neighborhood and gone down the slope towards the gas station. Anne sent me photos of the area.

On a following contact Anne made with Clyde, she "saw" that he was hiding somewhere in a small "junkyard" business. She feared he might have been attacked by one of the many coyotes in the area since we both sensed he had been in danger. She experienced his heart beating fast and his strong fear, and we both thought the worse. However, days later, she contacted him and learned that he had been with a cat friend when coyotes attacked and carried off his friend. Right now, at this writing, Clyde remains safely at large and still enjoying his life in the wild.

Some years into my practice, I experienced losing my cat, Peaches. We were living at the beach, and our house was elevated. The houses there are typically elevated at least twelve feet, and our cars were parked underneath. One late winter day, Peaches disappeared. Hans had opened the window in our office, and Peaches decided to go for an adventure. Even though it was winter, the temperatures were mild. However, we hadn't put the screens back on the windows. She had jumped the twelve feet to the ground below our office and disappeared. To make matters worse, the day turned from sunny and mild to stormy and cold. When I discovered Peaches's escape, I flew downstairs and called for her in the brewing storm with the wind howling and drowning out my voice. I felt so frustrated and helpless! I combed the little neighborhood frantically. I finally stopped the hysteria, stood still, and reminded myself that I was an animal communicator! I then did what I do daily with my lost animal clients, and I connected with Peaches.

She said, "Here I am," and showed me a pitch-black space.

It didn't help that she was also pitch-black herself, so I was very puzzled. But my intuitive skills kicked in and told me to turn around. At this point, I stood underneath the house where we park the cars. Behind me, four feet away, was our little bright yellow beach Jeep. The window was down, but the black vinyl top was up. The interior was pitch black, and from the little black boot behind the back seat looking straight at me, I saw two bright green eyes, the only thing of Peaches visible in the total blackness of that interior!

IS MY LOST ANIMAL STILL ALIVE?

Most communicators who opt out of doing lost animal cases do so because they find this question most troubling, and since it is often impossible to tell one way or another if an animal is alive or dead, this is where they call it quits. I remember my first serious blunder in this department. A young woman had left her small Chihuahua mix at her mother's house. The dog had gotten out of the yard through a hole in the fence. The woman called me, extremely upset and crying so hard she could hardly talk on the phone. I was able to accurately track her dog from the fence to a busy intersection nearby. At the intersection, the dog showed me a woman had stopped, gotten out of her car, and picked him up. The next thing the dog showed me was being taken into a vet's office. There the dog showed me that he was in some sort of cage, looking out around what looked like a surgical station. The dog seemed very much alive to me, but it turned out he had been hit by a car at the intersection, taken to the vet, and had died there. When I talked with the dog, he was probably in shock and did not comprehend his situation. This communication happened early in my career, and I did not have the experience to ask the right questions. And the dog couldn't tell me because he was processing his trauma and perhaps even deceased at that point.

When the girl found her dog had died, she called me on the phone in a thunderous rage, blaming me for the dog's death and a myriad of other sins. She informed me that she had cancelled her credit card, and I was not to charge her (I hadn't). The rage that came through her voice in that message was from extreme grief and feelings of abandonment, helplessness, and guilt. Some of us take a lot longer to mature, and we need to project our feelings onto others until that happens. I was her scapegoat. I'll confess this experience shocked me and taught me that I needed to be a lot more discerning about how I communicated with clients.

After getting over the shock of her attack, I took a good look at my approach to working with lost animals. If the animal doesn't know he's deceased, it can be hard for me to know. That's the first thing I had to admit. I could not blithely tell my client whether their animal was dead or alive; that was irresponsible. I have learned to tell my clients up front that I often cannot tell if the animal is in their body or not. If they're willing to work with me under those conditions, I promise them I will do my best.

The next lesson I needed to learn was that animals experiencing sudden death often don't care much about what just happened and take off in their spirit body. Before I was able to distinguish this spiritual state, I followed a number of animals as they went on grand adventures.

There was the Great Dane at a day care center who slipped away from his handler and went bounding into a spring rain-swollen, swift river that ran behind the center, leash trailing behind him. I followed him through the water and saw him struggling out of his leash and collar, climbing the banks downstream, and hitching a ride in a car full of family members back to town. The dog showed me road signs and topography that matched the landscape. He described a happy family and later the home they took him to and even the smells of their dinner cooking. However, the dog was found deceased a week later, tangled up in driftwood near the river's bank. The person I worked with understood because I had told her that I might have been following the dog's spirit, and the dog might not know he's deceased.

Since learning this important lesson, I've honed my skills, and there are times the animal will tell me something definite. Like the lost cat that showed me the last thing she remembered, which was a fox's face up close. Or the little dog that showed me the eagle talons as they descended on his body.

Wild animals and raptors do make up a good percentage of animal abductions, and the problem increases with time. Wild habitats are disappearing, and with them, food sources vanish. Raptors are in competition with coyotes in many areas. Coyote packs proliferate. In my practice, I notice that the animals most likely to abduct pets are owls, eagles, coyotes, and foxes. Their victims are usually cats and small dogs. I recently had a beautiful feral cat I was feeding carried off by a large raptor, probably an eagle.

But sometimes the animal friend wins. A client in Arizona called about her cat that had vanished some days before. I tracked the cat and discovered that she had been attacked by a coyote and was not moving. I could not tell if the cat was deceased. Often when an animal has passed away I'll experience a stillness and calmness around the animal. I'll sometimes see the animal sitting calmly near its body taking the world in, as if trying to get its bearings. But the animal also may have this same experience and be recovering and not fully in the body. I once watched a nature show in which a lioness had been bitten by a venomous snake, one that usually kills its victim. The filmmakers observed the cat for a full week, lying on the ground not moving. The cat was not dead. At the end of this long rest, the animal got up and moved on.

My client and I discussed the possibility that her friend was deceased. The cat seemed to be okay with its situation. About two weeks later, I received an excited phone call: The cat had returned, very skinny and with coyote-sized bite marks on its neck!

THE MOST AMAZING LOST ANIMAL STORY

All communicators have stand-out stories. This story unfolded over the course of many days as Barbara Rawson worked to recover her stolen dog, Sheeba. Barbara worked so hard to bring Sheeba home, and her story illustrates the rewards of launching a herculean effort towards recovering your lost loved one. Here's Barbara's story in her own words:

> *On December 31, 2004, our senior silver and black female German Shepherd dog, Sheeba, was dognapped while we were away from our home for a few hours. My husband, Randy; daughter, Miranda; son, Colby; and I searched for her with no luck. My daughter suggested we call Diane Samsel to get help. I asked Diane if we could meet in person, and she agreed.*
>
> *Miranda and I went to Diane's beach home with a drawing in hand of the area where we lived. Diane took a look at the drawing, which had no road names listed and no dwellings drawn, and immediately started telling us the names of the roads and describing a neighbor's land and multiple dwellings in detail. She said Sheeba had been taken by a man in a small reddish truck, that he had given her meat laced with tranquilizing drugs to make her compliant then put her in the back of his truck and took her to his home where he lived with his sister. She described the man in great detail and even told us what the young child at this man's house was feeding her . . . Cheerios. Diane heard a macaw-type bird in the background, heard someone speaking Spanish, and heard a gravel road very close by. She said Sheeba had been hearing us call for her.*
>
> *When Miranda and I got home, we told my husband what Diane told us. He is former military and immediately*

went into action launching a recon that night. We also called a private investigator, and the county police were contacted. We had no luck finding her that night, so the next day, we went over to the property where we suspected Sheeba was held. There were three trailers on the lot right next to a gravel road, just as Diane said there would be. We knocked on the doors of two trailers, but no answer. As we got to the third, we noticed pet carriers strewn about all over the yard marked with different people's last names. We knocked on the door, and a woman answered. We asked about our dog, and she told us she hadn't seen Sheeba. Her boyfriend walked up behind her, and they started speaking in Spanish. We heard a bird inside the home, and her little child came to see what was going on. It took everything I had to not break through them to check to see if Sheeba was there. Diane had warned that the people who had her were very dangerous.

That night, we spoke with Diane, and she said that Sheeba had been sold and moved elsewhere to be used in a dogfight that upcoming weekend. We collapsed. We felt helpless and sick to our stomachs. Diane said, "Put giant posters up with a large reward amount splashed across the top. Money makes people talk." I made the biggest sign I could and put it up directly in front of the driveway of the person we suspected, on the side of a very busy road. We put flyers everywhere. My PI, who is Hispanic, canvased the area and had been speaking to people who may know where Sheeba was. He was friends with the DA, and as soon as evidence was found, SLED [South Carolina Law Enforcement Division] was going to be called.

The next morning, which was a Thursday, I spoke with Diane, and she said, "Someone has released Sheeba!" Within an hour, I got a call that Sheeba had been spotted in the middle of a busy road. This is a dog that wouldn't go twenty feet from our house, and she was seen over a mile away. I got in my truck with Miranda, went down the road, saw a van with three people waving me down. Their van indicated they were service people, painters. We got out, and they said they saw her go into the woods.

Because I did not see Sheeba, and knowing we were up against dangerous people involved in dogfighting, I wondered if I could trust these people. I decided I could take down the two men if need be, and my daughter could easily handle the woman, so we headed out in the direction they were pointing with the three painters running right behind us. The five of us took off into the woods and arrived at a plowed field where we saw fresh dog tracks in the dirt. The tracks led us to a dirt road, quite a distance from the main road, I would guess a quarter mile, and that is when we saw a dog standing on a hill, but too far away to identify as ours. I was dry heaving at this point from not eating or drinking for days. Sheeba was a family member, and I was beside myself with anxiety and grief. When we got a little closer, it didn't look like Sheeba . . . we just couldn't be sure. I said, "I don't think it's her." Miranda said, "What if it is?" We took off running again.

The dog turned down another road and headed towards the busy road, well ahead of us. I was getting close to the road when I heard the car horns blowing. My stomach sank. When I reached the road, I begged the drivers to stop and stay at a standstill until I got this dog, even though I didn't know at the time whether it was Sheeba. Traffic stopped in both directions. As I slowly approached the dog, totally exhausted, I didn't recognize her, and she didn't recognize me. I kept hearing my daughter's voice saying, "What if it is her?" I got a car's length from her, and suddenly, we recognized each other, and in a second, I was laying on top of her in the middle of the road, sobbing. I called my husband to tell him what had happened and that we had Sheeba back. He sobbed. My son said he knew all along we would get her back.

Afterwards, I was contacted by two of the dogfighters saying that Sheeba had come to their home because she ran away from the fireworks. Lie. They just wanted to throw us off their scent. People were indeed talking.

The PI, Randy, and I went to Diane's home a few days later with a full map of the area. She was able to pinpoint on the map the area where Sheeba had been kept the last few days of her capture. The PI, who was a former police[man], flew over the area with the police and found the exact spot where Sheeba and other dogs had been kept: His report lead to the arrest of several people for dogfighting and enslavement of people.

A couple weeks later, Diane invited me to come to her amazing Animal Communication workshop in Tryon, NC, where I learned to speak with all species. She changed our lives, and we are forever grateful. She will always be supremely special in our hearts.

WHEN INSECTS DEMAND YOUR ATTENTION

Every living creature is here for a journey that is important not only to the creature herself but to the entire planet. Consider bees—if they weren't doing their work, humans would starve to death. Bees pollinate our crops. Insects are important, and I feel strongly about the demonization some of them suffer. Certainly disease-carrying insects are a major threat to us, and we need to avoid them. Infestations are a manifestation of nature out of balance. Stink bugs came into the country and were a problem until birds and other creatures learned that they were a food source.

Right now as I write, there's a new tick species infestation that is causing dramatic problems.

Insects in an out-of-balance environment can be a nightmare for humans. However, it isn't because they're evil; it's because they can remind us of our own fragility in an out-of-balance world. The insects themselves taught me to consider the frustrations of their situation.

We moved to the Charleston, South Carolina area in 1998 to a small barrier island. Our little home was up on pilings as is necessary when living at sea level, and the yard was a pleasant, sandy affair that abutted a small lagoon boasting not only herons and turtles but also alligators. Spanish moss graced the old oak that grew behind the deck—a tree that seemed to be home to dozens of creatures that included raccoon, heron, and snake. The property was alive with wildlife, and I was in heaven. My animal communication practice was in its first years, and my office over-looked this coastal wonderland. A great blue heron often fished at the banks of the little lagoon, and smaller herons graced the limbs of the oak. Hans enjoyed catching tiny fish with his cast net from the lagoon. Rusty, our tame feral cat enjoyed devouring these little spiny creatures whole and watched patiently from the porch as Hans did his fishing for him.

But there was a devil in this paradise: the fire ant. I made their acquaintance by accident on our first full day in the little cottage. When I awoke that first morning after moving in, I stumbled sleepily into the kitchen to make coffee only to see little tiny ants all over the counter. I have had ants in my homes in the past, and the insects didn't bother me. I didn't use professional insecticides, but I did go about discouraging the insects so they would take up housekeeping elsewhere. Infestations were never a problem. So I gently began wiping ants off the counter, talking with them all the while about setting up elsewhere. Suddenly ants crawled all over my hand and at a signal bit me simultaneously. Ouch!!!! After calming down and backing off, I did a little research on the consciousness I had just encountered. It was the fire ant! I had heard about this invasive species and had been a bit in awe of its social power, and here it was challenging me firsthand (literally). My arms were covered with tiny red blisters.

As an animal communicator, I felt that I needed to reach out and try to settle this matter with my animal communication skills. I first contacted the queen of this fire ant colony that had invaded my kitchen. She was a fierce spirit and full of fight. Her chief concern was securing territory for their food supply. All properties surrounding ours used aggressive chemical attacks on them, and she felt her colony's life was under constant threat. I explained the human perspective and the pain her colony inflicted on humans with their aggression. She was not concerned with my plight, and I realized her awareness was that of a being that felt threatened and under attack. She was unable to process the needs of another species, much less care about us. I decided to design a truce that would address her need for food and safe territory.

I had an old bag of Power Paws, the pet food supplement I manufacture, and told her I'd place some of it daily in a specific place on the property if she'd agree to leave the house. When her colony members got a taste of the Power Paws, she was happy and accepted the arrangement. We lived happily together for a number of months—not bothered by the fire ants during that period. Then one day, they reappeared. I reached out again to the queen of the colony only to find that she and her tribe had been defeated in battle by another colony. My fire ant queen had been replaced by another fire ant queen. I set about making the same deal with this queen, and things settled into place as before: But not for long. Fire ant matters on the property had devolved into the insect version of World War III. Since we offered food and a safe territory, word had swiftly spread through the little barrier island that we were prime real estate. Territorial battles ensued, and our property became a fire ant war zone. At this point, eradication became necessary.

As this event unfolded during the first years of my practice, I wonder if I might have better skills available for dealing with the problem now. The fire ant consciousness I dealt with then was focused on only one thing—survival and expansion. This consciousness had no intention to live in harmony. It was a ferocious being of steely determination. I was naïve at that point and believed that a win-win situation was always possible. But in the face of a desperate species that could be dangerous if provoked, I now know that until the fire ant is better domesticated, they will be in continual battle with humans. I wish them well.

I mentioned earlier that I once had arachnophobia. People have irrational fears of different creatures of this world. Years ago I made a project of overcoming my phobia. I read as much about spiders as I could. I bought a beautiful hand-painted T-shirt depicting a variety of colorful spiders and wore it regularly. I meditated next to webs with big spiders in the center. I made myself talk with Spider and appreciate her beauty and purpose. At our beach house, I adopted a spider totem, the golden silk orb weaver spider, and within a few weeks, we had a necklace of the webs around the house with big, long gold spiders hanging in the center. According to shamanistic tradition, the appearance of animals in your life or in your dreams is symbolic. Animals are messengers from the spirit world. For me, watching the golden orb constantly reweaving her web reminded me that every day is a new adventure which, for Hans and me, was certainly true of our time together in that little beach cottage.

After the beach, we moved to the mountains of North Carolina. During remodeling, we discovered an infestation of black widow spiders. I decided to live in harmony with these shy and reclusive creatures as they were tucked away and out of sight. I admire them for their beauty and respect their threat.

One day, while cleaning the French doors in our living room, I came across a large female black widow backed into a corner of the window. What she was doing there was a mystery. It wasn't her nest area as it was exposed to light. Maybe she was hunting or hurt. I communicated to her that I meant her no harm and would need to relocate her. I found a jar and piece of cardboard to accomplish the task, but in the process of relocating her, I accidently killed her. I felt sick to my stomach and apologized to her spirit for being so careless. These magnificent creatures come into our lives and bring us something important. Their presence is a totem of the spirit they carry.

At the time of this incident, I was working through a turbulent relationship with my stepdaughter, who was going through extremely difficult times in her life and was testing her father and me in ways that were very painful. The spider taught me that the darker thoughts and feelings inherent in our relationship could become destructive for both of us. Soon after the spider encounter, my stepdaughter had a tragic accident. To this day, I regret that I was unable to create a loving relationship with this beautiful human, as she had a magnificent spirit and tremendous potential—all senselessly cut short before she had a chance to find herself.

You will often experience times when you know the animal and insect world is communicating directly with you. For instance, the cardinal, my mother's totem, becomes ridiculously abundant at those times when I know my mother is close in spirit. She passed in 2016 at the age of ninety-six but visits us regularly. I know she's around when those gorgeous red birds mob my deck and feeders. My mother was known for the smiles and cheer she brought with her when she came into people's lives, and I can feel her beaming at me as I watch the cardinals.

Once, at a very joyous time, I walked on the beach near Charleston, SC, surrounded by thousands of migrating dragonflies. At that time in my life, I was painting and showing and selling my art, enjoying an abundance of creative energy. The wondrous presence of those dragonflies perfectly captured the essence of my happiness.

Everyone in this house (except the cats) respects the life of the insects. We have to manage the termites, which we do, but we are never bothered by the spiders and will remove them as gently as possible wherever their presence becomes an issue. We capture and release outside all crawling, flying, and stinging beings. I have a good relationship with ants and have not been bothered by them here. A few scouts may come into the house now and then. I tell them there's nothing here for them, and usually they will leave in a reasonable amount of time.

Mosquitoes don't seem to bother us. We use herbal sprays while gardening. I will suck on an herbal mint lozenge during gnat season and one well-directed puff of mint breath usually discourages them from hanging around my face.

Several years ago, I was leading a workshop on a ranch not far from Austin, Texas. It was a wild and wonderful property, and my hostess had an impressive scorpion population living in her home. When they appeared in the house, she would scoop them up with a piece of cardboard and fling them outside, where her chickens, knowing the routine well, would make snacks out of their little black arachnid bodies. I chose to adopt her nonchalance when the first scorpion dropped onto my lap. I gingerly brushed him aside, and he went about his business as I did mine. However, when I awoke the next morning, I had seven scorpion bites on my back, arranged in an uncanny spiral reminiscent of a scorpion's tail! It hurt a bit, and the bite spots turned into little blisters that itched and burned but otherwise I survived.

Scorpion reminds us of life's important transformational moments. Astrologically, the sign of Scorpio introduces us to times in our lives when we need to release one way of being in order to follow a better path in life. My scorpion friend was giving me a reminder. My natal chart's Moon occupies the sign of Scorpio. Moon in Scorpio is comfortable with depth and intensity. After the scorpion bites, my work did take on more emotional depth and intensity. However, at times transformation can be chaotic, and the introduction to this energy certainly felt that way!

WHAT ABOUT SNAKES?

My Aunt Betty was terrified of snakes. My earliest memory of her was seeing her passed out on the dining room floor of our apartment in Lubbock, Texas. I was five, and she had come for a visit. Texas has incredible rattlesnakes, and I'm sure Aunt Betty knew about them. My father pranked her by putting a rubber snake on the floor right outside the kitchen door and then called her out of the kitchen, where she was cooking dinner with my mother. The next thing I remember was her bloodcurdling scream and then the sight of her sprawled out on the floor. My father thought it was hilarious, my mother was furious, and I was dumbstruck by the sight of one of my favorite people in such a heap, felled by something I thought was so harmless. Today I look back on this scene and think my father was a jerk, but he and his friends (mostly army buddies) were always doing insane things they thought were funny. This is how it is to grow up in a family when your parents aren't much older than you are…psychologically.

I have never been afraid of snakes, ever. On the ranch, we loved finding little garter snakes to handle. These snakes felt wonderful to us as they wriggled in our hands, and they provided us with one of the unusual experiences that I think all children should enjoy. The snakes would always poop on our hands, and the smell was horrible yet thrilling in its ferocity. Now I realize they must have been terrified of us, and rightly so. Some kids could be cruel, but my grandparents taught us to value all animals. Except moles— those were never welcome in their gardens. Out walking in the fields surrounding the farm one day, my grandpa captured a big bumblebee in his hand and held it up to my ear for me to hear. The moment was a delightful communication with my mostly silent, sweet grandfather. He opened his hand and the bumblebee lumbered off, continuing her journey. My grandfather loved these poetic gestures when sharing his connection with nature.

Once walking in Hitchcock Woods, a twelve-hundred-acre equestrian park in the middle of Aiken, SC, I walked up to a long and fat rattlesnake sunning himself on a little bridge built over low-lying swamp area. Thrilled to be in the company of such a snake, I sat on my haunches about three feet from the snake, admiring his beauty and enjoying the power he radiated. My walking partner stood about fifteen feet away quietly trying to coax me away from the beast. I knew in that moment that the snake would not harm me—he was as comfortable having me admire him as I was doing the admiring. This event happened when I was in my early thirties. I was not a communicator then but could get into physical spaces with animals in which I sensed a perfect oneness. This was one of those moments. My partner, on the other hand, was sweating profusely after I rejoined him on the path. He told me I was an idiot. Maybe so, but I cherish that moment with the snake, and it was worth any risk involved.

I was out hiking the Shut-In Trail near Asheville, North Carolina, with my husband years ago when I came close to stepping on a snake sunning himself on the path. He was practically invisible, and yet, I sensed him and lengthened my stride just enough that my footfall landed about an inch from his body. My husband saw this maneuver and congratulated me. The snake slid off to safer grounds. Maybe it was just luck, but I think that my respect for snakes keeps me in good stead with them.

Last summer I was gardening when I stepped right next to a juvenile cottonmouth. He became incensed by this near miss and began to charge me—mouth open and looking about ten times bigger than he was. He then headed in the direction to our "Catio" (an outdoor structure our cats have access to for their safe enjoyment of the great outdoors). Knowing that this little snake would be seen as something irresistible by the cats, I attempted to divert him to an open space. Instead, he headed again at me with his little white mouth open flashing his little fangs. I had frightened and angered him, and he was attacking me. And fast. Alas, the snake lost. I felt terrible about this encounter. The adrenalin from seeing him head for the Catio had kept me from thinking clearly. I could have relocated him. He could have become familiar with what was safe around the garden, and he would have probably left us alone. But in the moment, my animal communicator self was not in control.

Snake gave me a warning with that encounter. Snakes represent another form of transformative energy similar to Scorpion. Snakes shed their skins when they grow and develop. This benign encounter with a dangerous snake reminded me that I needed to wake up and shed something fundamental about the way I was behaving in order to grow. I looked at my life and relationships and indeed found that to be true. I examined whether always pleasing others was a healthy choice for me and determined that I needed to be more assertive. Sometimes showing one's "fangs" (constructively, of course) can be a necessary course of action! The process of change is often difficult and scary, but Snake jolted me into action and there was no turning back. I made the changes and am now a much stronger person.

A number of years ago, I hosted a shamanic workshop on the little barrier island where we were planning to build our home. Kenn Day delivered his wonderful Post-Tribal Shamanism seminar, and afterward, we took him in our golf cart (no cars allowed) to show him around the island. During the course of our tour, I told Kenn about some recent problems that the islanders were experiencing with their governance. It was nothing serious, but I was curious if there were any animal energies out of balance that could be behind the difficulties. Kenn thought about it for a minute or so and told me that Snake and Eagle spirits were fighting on the island.

I thought this over for a minute and came to the conclusion that this might explain why some residents who were more idealistic and visionary (eagle) were at odds with the residents who tended to be more practical and down-to-earth (snake). I parked the golf cart at a beach access, and as our little party began to walk the boardwalk out to the beach, an eagle descended from a dead tree to our left, flew across our path, and scooped a snake off the ground to our right! The eagle flew back to his perch on the dead tree and devoured the snake. I interpreted the event as a good omen. To me it signaled that the idealistic (Eagle) members of the island would prevail by taking in and digesting more practical ideas (Snake). Our little touring party was in awe of the whole experience, and I thanked the great spirit of the island for talking to us so clearly through the animals living there.

STORIES FROM ANIMALS OF THE WATERS

CAT CRUSHERS

When we first moved to the Charleston, South Carolina area, Hans and I rented a small cottage in Wild Dunes on Isle of Palms. We were hunkered down for the process of building our dream house on Dewees Island, the barrier island directly north of Isle of Palms. We enjoyed Sunday mornings on the screened-in porch reading *The New York Times* and drinking coffee. In the live oaks towering over our little beach cabin, great blue herons kept vigil over the pond behind us. Small alligators sunned on the banks, and golfers motored by on the opposite side, chasing their tiny white balls.

The cats were thoroughly entertained by the wildlife and endless stream of happy golfers. We had trained them all to be indoor cats by telling them of the "Cat Crusher." When they rushed the doors as youngsters, I would stomp my foot and yell, "Cat Crusher!" I started this regimen by explaining to them that cat crushers were unseen creatures who come out of nowhere, attack, and leave their bodies all broken up so they can't be used. I'll admit the image I projected to them during this training period was gruesome, and they responded with appropriate revulsion, but it was effective in getting the point across. I wanted them to associate the act of dashing out the front or back door with something scary. This training usually took a few months. After a while, they stopped rushing the door, knowing that danger lurked outside.

One night shortly after the training began, Buster woke me up—he was just a few years old at the time. He was excited and jumped from the bed and rushed over to the cat door installed in our room and then rushed back to the bed, all the while telling me that he could see the Cat Crushers. It was a balmy, clear full moon evening, and when I got up and followed him out to the screened-in porch, I saw the other four cats lined up at the far edge of the screen looking down towards the little lagoon, motionless and stiff with excitement. I joined them at the edge of the porch and looked down to see several little three-foot-long alligators sleeping on the bank in the bright moonlight. It was indeed the Cat Crushers! I congratulated the cats on their find and confirmed that those were, indeed, cat crushers. We never had to worry about our cats sneaking out an open door again.

OCTOPUS

One Sunday morning, not long after the Cat Crusher episode, an octopus in peril reached out to me. Deeply absorbed in the real estate section of *The New York Times*, I suddenly had to put the paper down as I realized I was experiencing a strong need to travel to Dewees! At the time I didn't know it was a call for help. All I knew was that I had to respond. I told Hans we needed to go to Dewees, and soon. I had no idea where I'd gotten the compulsion to abandon our leisurely morning and embark on a quest, objective unknown.

We dressed, drove to the ferry landing, boarded the ferry to Dewees, and arrived on the island an hour later. We kept a golf cart and a kayak on the island. We hooked our kayak to the golf cart and headed to the north end of the island. Again, I had no idea why I was so compelled to move in this direction. On the northern shore of the island, a ten-minute golf cart ride from the landing, we launched the kayak and began to paddle across the narrow but choppy channel that separated Dewees from Bull Island, an undeveloped barrier island directly north. The beach at the southernmost tip of the island is vast, bordered with the skeletons of the maritime forest decimated years earlier by Hurricane Hugo. We pulled the kayak onto the deserted beach, and I hopped out and headed to the beach's tidal pools left when the tide receded hours before.

Without thinking, I traveled to one shallow pool in particular and stopped in my tracks when I looked down and saw a little orange octopus lying at the bottom. He was clearly stressed by the receding water level of his tiny pool and had been sending signals all morning. To this day I don't know how I picked up his distress call but I did. Such is the life of an intuitive. I carefully picked up the little guy and walked him over to the water's edge of the inlet and released him to his home. I felt his gratitude and the gratitude of Octopus Spirit and to this day feel a deep connection to the species.

THE "BOSS" FISH

My good friend Heidi Vanderbilt and I were visiting the Chihuly exhibit at the Biltmore in Asheville, NC. The estate has a beautiful Italian garden that features three formal ponds where a lot of the colorful glass sculptures floated or were anchored in the water. In the bright September sun, we lingered by the biggest of these formal water features and watched the koi swim up to us, regard us briefly, and then swim away. I began a conversation with the fish and was told that their interest in us was for food only. They told me that humans come and feed them but that most of the humans didn't feed them, so they were always busy trying to sort out who had food. They watched as we humans came and went, hoping for tasty morsels. I don't know the feeding schedule of the

Biltmore fish, but I was shown by the fish that people dressed in uniforms and wearing rubber boots tended the ponds. The fish had a great interest in these people because of the food.

While we were admiring the languid movements of the koi, I noticed a large black and silver fish approaching me. Beneath his darker coloring shown a brilliant gold—he projected a powerful presence, and as he approached me, he demanded my attention as he stated clearly, "I am the boss fish."

Experience has taught me that when animals use a particular word to describe themselves, like "boss," it means a human has given them that name. I will never forget Heidi's Arabian mare, Delight, telling me when I first communicated with her that her nickname was Twinkletoes. I mentioned this to Heidi who informed me that she never called Delight by that name. Weeks later Heidi sent an email to tell me she had just found out a good friend of hers, who rides with her, had been calling Delight Twinkletoes when Heidi was out of earshot!

So it was with Mr. Boss Fish—he had a friend on staff who had given him that name. I asked him what had elevated him to his position. He said once he knew the pond, he was boss and that the human had recognized this truth. He explained that he knew that he was in a pond and that the humans took care of it. The other fish didn't know this. They did not possess this level of awareness. His human friend had recognized him as being special and gave him his title, of which he was proud. Animals gain awareness the same way we humans do, by expanding their perspective on the world around them. They grow in consciousness by having the courage to accept something new beyond what they know—by pushing their boundaries through listening, learning, believing, and then mastering a world beyond their prior understanding.

In mastering the energy of the pond, he had become the biggest presence swimming with the other koi. He said all of the other fish recognized his position and that he helped them when he could. I asked him to tell me about his fish community. He told me that the community was well cared for and that there were few hungry or sick fish. He said the biggest problem could be territorial issues. Sometimes fish would have special places where they liked to be still and quiet. If another fish intruded on them, there would be a problem. I asked if there were any bullies in his community. He said no. Bullies are fish in trouble, and the pond didn't have that often, but when a fish did get in trouble, the people who fed them took care of that fish.

I asked him what he liked most about people, and he said he enjoyed the laughter, smiles, and admiration his community members gave him. He said that people have beautiful colors around them and that the children, the smaller ones, are brilliant. I asked him how it was to have the Chihuly exhibit placed in his home, and he said it was frightening because no one explained what would happen, but once his friend came to feed him, he knew they would all be okay. He showed me the installation of the sculptures with all of the rubber boots in the water and all the fear and chaos those boots created. "Too many," he said. I admired him for a few moments, taking in his big energy, and then he swam slowly away from me, off to greet his next human. He knows his pond, and he's getting to know humans. He's a good ambassador from the fish world.

WORKING WITH HEALTH DILEMMAS IN ANIMALS

When called to consult about a health issue, I make it clear I am not a vet and cannot counter any recommendations given by a vet. Knowing if the animal has had a recent blood panel drawn by the vet is important as is finding out if the animal is on any medications. Having established these boundaries, I explain to my human client that I work as an empath and report only the energetic sensations I pick up from scanning the animal's body. I also pick up information from what the animal tells me when I ask about sensations I feel.

In my experience, stoicism in animals is a primary defense mechanism, and animals often won't show their discomfort or body issues. I've seen that they have developed a natural way to "leave their body" when pain gets too intense. For instance, the rapid panting often displayed by injured animals seems to bring some relief. I learned this lesson at age nine when our family's young boxer dog Tawny was hit by a car. I heard the collision and ran into the street to see her lying howling in the road, her leg broken.

She cried at first but then began a rapid panting, and I witnessed in amazement that she was beginning to relax. I was hysterical and naturally held my breath between sobs. The grown-ups had a harder time with me than with our family dog. Tawny healed rapidly and even learned to climb fences, chasing squirrels with a cast on her leg! When I look back on the incident, I admire how she took care of her body during that crisis, and I also recall with some embarrassment how I fell apart.

Native Americans taught their children to be stoic as did German farmers before modern times. In Germany it was called "hardening," and today it would probably be called child abuse. When I read my family history in a book named *The Sorting of Samsels*, one of my relatives wrote about the practice of hardening used by my ancestors.[5] Growing up I was a bit of a hypochondriac, but the minute I went to the doctor I clammed up, telling them that nothing was wrong with me. My mother would audibly groan at this point in the consultation. Sometimes that's how it is with my animal clients. Some won't want to let me know what's going on in their bodies. But when I discover a sore spot, they usually will want to tell me something about it.

When I work empathically with animals, sensing the energy in their bodies, I can report back to my client what I pick up. I do this by focusing on pathways of energy called meridians. Meridian pathways form the basis of traditional Chinese medicine, TCM. Meridians run throughout a body, and each meridian is associated with an organ. I have learned to feel which meridians are running extra-strong energy, usually indicative of a problem or stress in the corresponding organ. There is an excellent book on the subject for our purposes: *Four Paws, Five Directions: A Guide to Chinese Medicine for Cats and Dogs* by Cheryl Schwartz, DVM.[6] A battered copy is shelved within reaching distance of my desk.

Recently I was communicating with a dog that kept pawing at her mouth and was limping. The abscessed tooth her guardian told me about was easy to sense as a pain in the lower jaw. But the limp worried her as she thought it might be arthritis. When I followed the meridian, I could feel the large Intestines meridian that went down the left side of the dog's face, past the spot where the abscess was, and continued down the shoulder and left leg, terminating in the foot.

In Chinese medicine, the organs are paired, and the lung is paired with the large intestines. I know from experience that grief is often a factor in problems with these paired organs. I asked the dog if she had been sad recently, and she said she had lost her friend (her mate had died), and she missed him. When I reported this to the guardian, she confirmed that was true. I asked her if the abscessed tooth came after the death of the friend and she said yes. Then I suggested that the limp would probably clear up once the tooth was fixed because the dog was very sensitive on that left paw, where the meridian terminated. I did not feel the sharp pain and heat I usually feel associated with inflammation when an animal has arthritis. My client emailed a few weeks later to confirm that after the abscess was treated, her dog was back to her normal self, not limping at all.

Sometimes animals develop health issues as a result of being pushed too hard by their owner. For instance, it has been my experience that lameness in horses most often arises in early training, when the trainer is not in partnership with the horse and demands too much, too early. These trainers believe the "one size fits all" approach. Some animals need more time to mature. I have a client whose brilliant horse was not doing well in training. I asked the horse what he needed and got the picture of a green pasture with his friends grazing nearby. I told my client that the horse needed some time out. She put him out in the pasture that season, and when he went back into training the next season, he loved his work and did well.

BONDS AND THE HEALING POWER OF BEING HEARD

Not long ago I communicated with a dog on the West Coast, an eleven-year-old golden retriever. In the consultation, I found that there were structural issues in the dog's sacrum, which needed physical therapy and perhaps chiropractic attention—those issues were easy to address. A deeper problem, difficult to diagnose, had settled in his stomach. I could feel a spot in the stomach that felt hot and inflamed but not what I've come to know as a "cancerous" feel. The dog's guardian confirmed that the dog had been refusing food off and on.

In my practice, I find that if I synch with the animal's pain and at the same time ask the animal about the pain, I can get stories tied to an emotional wound that has settled into the affected area. This dog had suffered the loss of an important older dog several years prior and had never gotten over the loss, so deep were their bonds of friendship. The deceased dog friend had been aging and had died suddenly, and my client dog could not understand what had happened as no one had explained the death to her. She felt abandoned and afraid. Her fear turned into anger, which she hid from herself, and eventually that anger had settled into the tissue of her stomach. As I kept the empathic bond and talked with her, she began to share her long-suppressed feelings of grief with me. And as she grieved, I could feel wave after wave of relief wash over her body. Healing often begins with the release of this type of emotional trauma.

The bonds that tie us to those we love are potent. They create substantive links from one body to another, links that transmit currents of information that are emotional, physical, and spiritual in nature. For instance, when I work with lost animals, I suggest my human client actively send out a "golden cord" from their heart to the heart of the animal that is missing. I instruct the human to then send their lost friend thoughts of being reunited. This cord already exists in the relationship bond, but this exercise seems to reinforce the bond, reminding each to keep connected. This strengthened bond creates synchronicities that work to reunite partners lost to one another. I also believe that guardian angels have a lot to do with the process once you're able to manifest from the heart space.

I work often with these bonds in my practice. For over thirteen years, I've practiced a technique called Voice Dialogue. Voice Dialogue is the name given to a therapy created by Doctors Hal and Sidra Stone in California. They developed the technique in their psychoanalytical practices over a number of years of working together. In a nutshell, the practice posits that each personality is made of sub-personalities that have their own perspective and often work independently of the "operating ego"—the part of the personality that chooses which personality/perspective will be functioning at any given time.

These personalities can independently form bonds with others in order to get their needs met—with the operating ego having little or no control over the process. These can be controlling, codependent, negative, or positive bonds to characterize a few. Bonds are created when we disown a part of ourselves and "hire" others to carry those parts for us. A simple example would be sports figures. We want to enjoy athletics and adore our sports heroes. Those heroes often carry our projected desires and dreams of physical skill, strength, and prowess. If you've ever been to a team sports event, you know how powerful the bonds are between the team players and their fans! That bond can seem physical at times.

We project these bonds onto our animal friends too! The heart bonds between human and animal are wonderful and healing. But frustrating bonds exist that can be destructive and wounding because they are unconscious and usually arise from unfinished childhood issues involving pain, abandonment, and betrayal.

To work with a bond that may be unproductive, you need to understand its dynamics. In the case of a dysfunctional bond, a human in a relationship with her animal is carrying a self that may be under-functioning or disowned. The person then projects that self onto their beloved animal friend. We begin the healing process by identifying the projected self or selves and naming it. For example, we may have disowned a self that could be called "the tyrant" and projecting it onto our new pit bull puppy. Anytime the little puppy shows any tyrant tendencies, we react strongly because we do not like the tyrant we carry. Pretty soon the puppy learns that acting the tyrant brings plenty of attention, and suddenly you have a tyrannical grown pit bull to contend with in public. Not good!

The next step is to treat each personality part within the bond as a unique individual with his or her own strong perspective. This is done by physically naming the part of the personality as we just did for the tyrant. Another self that's common is "the rebel."

The following is an example of how I use this technique to resolve difficult issues with our animal companions. The rebel was a self that manifested as a horse that wouldn't go into the trailer and resisted all trailering efforts in a recent communication I had with its frustrated human. After talking with the horse to get her perspective and then talking with the human, I discovered that the human couldn't abide her own rebellious nature, and so every time her horse reacted by balking, she exhibited a strong reaction—thinking the horse's behavior was rebellious. In truth, the horse was confused.

In the case of the horse not going into the trailer, it was not a fear issue for the horse; it was a clash of opinions stemming from the horse not feeling respected. There was no dialogue in the transaction; the human was expecting rebellion because that's what she feared would happen, and that's what manifested. This case is based on a client who contacted me who was at her wit's end about the problem. In the session, I asked the client to *become* the rebellious part of the horse and talk with me as though she was experiencing exactly what the horse experienced. This effort requires coming to terms with the need to control as opposed to seeking a solution through dialogue. When I talked to my client *as the rebellious horse*, she immediately sensed the problem from the horse's perspective. She knew in an instant how she was creating the problem and how to fix the problem.

During the course of speaking from her horse's perspective, she began to realize that she had deeply buried rebellious feelings herself. Growing up, in order to be a "good girl," she had learned to obey rules and be nice about following the wishes of others. Her horse was carrying the disowned part of her personality that did not want to follow orders! She felt embarrassed at first then laughed and then embraced that part of herself. Now that she was grown up, she was free to do what she wanted and could let go of that childlike part of her that she was clearly seeing as her horse's problem.

The horse, from his perspective, was balking at loading into the trailer because he sensed there was something *wrong*. Horses, being prey animals, look for predators everywhere, and he was sure there might be a mountain lion on board that trailer! Why else would his trusted person be telegraphing her tension to him if not to warn him that the trailer might not be safe? When I discussed what was going on with his person and clarified the situation, he felt quite relieved. In this transaction, there was dialogue and respect. My client reported later that the trailering problems vanished after that one conversation.

Communication difficulties arising from the need to control instead of trust lead to unhappy relationships. There is within the bond between humans and animals a need to come to terms with the necessities of living together. The human, being a lot more in control of the environment than the animal, has the upper hand in most life situations. With good early training and mutual respect, the animal and human come to workable terms with all of the vagaries of cohabitation. With an open heart, trust, and patience both partners enjoy their relationship. That is the ideal. But what happens when one of us is being just a little "neurotic"?

The parent/child relationship we experience with our companion animal friend offers us the opportunity to grow beyond our unresolved childhood issues. We love and care for our animals as we were loved and cared for by our parents. My cat Buster was my heart. He was funny, beautiful, gracious, generous, and totally self-absorbed. Just like my mother! These are the things I loved about her. Buster kept his spirit high up until his final hour—just as Mom did when she passed away at age ninety-six. Buster was always curious about the adventure that was just around the corner. And so it was with my dearly departed mother. Often we live our parental ideals through our animals. Losing Buster (he was ready to leave his body at age seventeen) coincided with my own personal need to grow beyond the idealized version I held for my mother.

I think the need to grow spiritually, to grasp ever-higher

spiritual realities is one of our purposes on this planet. Our animals can help us with that process. I believe that when we release immature bonds, our parent or parents also experience the release, even if they are in spirit. Animals tell me that they are in service to us. They serve by cooperating with our deepest agendas, reflecting back to us without judgment our true nature. They serve as our guides by helping us to become conscious of the parts of our being that need to be perfected so that we can be the best we can be in a relationship. When Buster went to spirit, we had agreed that he was free to explore other incarnations— our work together was complete.

It's important to recognize how we project our needs and psychological complexes onto our animal relationships. In the process of owning your projections, you can develop skills that help you see into the true nature of your animal friend. This is often the first step towards clarity in communication.

I recently had an eighty-one-year-old man as a client who was grieving the loss of his cat, Sweetheart. She had passed about six months prior, and my client could not get over feeling she was still suffering from the disease that finally took her body at age sixteen. When Sweetheart talked with me, it was clear that she was in a space of divine love and was staying close in spirit to her human to give him comfort while he grieved. The suffering he thought she felt was the suffering he was experiencing and was unable to process from his own recent illnesses as well as losing her. In our session, I communicated his beloved cat's compassion, love, and devotion while pointing out that even though she had been ill, she was able to transcend her illness and enjoy her life right up to the end. Animals are stoic and know how to rise above uncomfortable conditions. Sweetheart focused on the devotion of their bond and took only the joy of their relationship with her to sprit. Human guilt is an emotion animals that are in spirit have a hard time understanding.

At the end of that session, I could feel the client's heart lighten as he embraced and moved through his own grief and saw clearly that his friend was in a place of joy. At moments like this, I see the truth in the saying that "death is an illusion."

MORE ON THE HEAL- ING POWER OF ANIMAL COMMUNICATION

When sessions involve complex family dynamics, a communication session with the animals in the family often brings changes that benefit all family members. One session can often resolve a full spectrum of difficult emotions that may plague family dynamics. I enter these sessions knowing that there is probably an abundance of love and care already in place. People don't call me unless they trust themselves and the universe on a deep level. They want to know the deepest thoughts and desires of their animal companions and are not afraid of what they might hear. Here is a story that illustrates the process of healing through communication:

Kim Caldwell called from Greenville, South Carolina about her one-year-old kittens, Pete and Repeat. The solid black kittens had become a loving part of the family. They were littermates, and Pete was wonderfully playful with Repeat, the female and runt of the litter, who was extraordinarily lovable. Then the family adopted a six-month-old Rottweiler puppy named Thor who proceeded to terrorize the kittens with his outsized sense of fun and rambunctiousness, which turned into a nasty game of "stalk the kitties." The kittens in return showed their stress by peeing outside the litter box. In my practice and in my life with many cats, I've found that peeing outside of the litter box often denotes fear-based stress. In this case, the fear was visceral; the puppy began stalking them as prey.

Kim contacted me, and I talked with the kittens and the puppy. The kittens communicated their fears, and the puppy communicated his enjoyment of having two prey creatures to play with. It was a pretty cut and dried situation. I then turned my attention to Kim and asked her if the puppy was being trained to treat the kittens with respect. It turned out that his outrageous and aggressive game had made him the center of attention, and he loved every minute of it. His bully behavior had gotten out of control. In talking with Thor, I realized he was a pleaser; he wants people to like him.

Well-trained before arriving as the newest family member, he was a dream puppy in all respects. However, he could not resist the fun of watching those two black fuzzy things scatter when he charged them. It was a game he enjoyed. I communicated with him how important it was to learn to get along with Pete and Repeat. I let him know how upsetting his behavior was to them and that Kim was upset too.

I then explained to Kim that the family needed to monitor Thor and make sure he isn't allowed to bully the kittens. When I concluded the session, I could feel the relief not only from Kim but also from the animal members of the family. I'm certain Thor was aware of the distress he was causing but the fun of the game and the fact he wasn't being trained away from the behavior made it too tempting to give up on his own.

Shortly after this session, I received a wonderful email from Kim letting me know what happened afterward:

The evening after I talked to you, we had a family meeting between our four kids, me, and hubs to relay all that you had shared. We discussed how Thor was being a bully to the kittens, how this has made Pete and Repeat feel, etc. My family immediately changed their ways, unanimously! My husband led the charge with apologizing to the cats for how he had let his puppy be the bully, loved on the kittens, and reassured them that that was not going to happen anymore.

Now, every night, we make sure that Thor sees us

playing with the kittens (as well as sweet Marla, our older dog) and reprimand Thor when he tries to pick on them. You would not believe the transformation it has made. Not only have we not had ONE SINGLE MESS in the house since then (changing from one to two times daily to no messes in two weeks), but the animals are finally beginning to coexist. I looked over in our living room last night, and all four animals were laying down in the same living space. NEVER has that ever happened before.

Like I mentioned to you on the phone, it gives me great peace to know that I have you available to our family as a resource, and I so appreciate the ability to call you when I need you! Thank you for being a blessing to our whole family . . . animal and human alike.

The above story is an example of how animal communication can heal family patterns. The spiritual bonds in this family are strong, and the respect they have for their animal family members is a reflection of that bond.

A very recent case involved an elderly, thirteen-year-old male cat I'll call Cocoa. Cocoa had stopped eating regularly and had gone from weighing twelve pounds to weighing only eight pounds in just a matter of months. A vet check revealed nothing amiss in his blood work. He was given an appetite stimulant. Cocoa's human guardian called me and expressed her frustration and sadness at her beloved companion's decline. She felt great affection for him and wanted to help him resolve his suffering. Here, I am using "suffering" in the sense of an ordeal one is undergoing. As I came to understand his situation, Cocoa was undergoing a transformation from "in his body" to "not in his body" as best he knew how. Since he was not sick in the classical way—no cancer or any other disease that animals manifest at the end of life—I came to the conclusion that his choice to leave his body arose from an emotional issue.

During the session, Cocoa hid out under my human client's

bed. I made contact with him and relayed to his guardian that Cocoa was a peacekeeper at heart and didn't like dissent around him—something was bothering him. During our exchange, he was stoic and initially not forthcoming with information. However, I picked up a strong need to be number one. He was listening and began to trust me more. He then began to open up and told me he was being bullied. My client confirmed that she had a seven-year-old male cat that enjoyed pushing Cocoa around. I then did an empathic check of Cocoa's body. When I entered his thoracic area, I felt a strong constriction in the upper part of his lungs. A wave of grief washed over me, and I asked my client if he'd suffered a loss shortly before his health issues arose. She confirmed that a female cat he was fond of had died at about the same time that Cocoa's health issues started.

I proceeded with my "empathic" checkup to the organs of digestion and found that his stomach felt hot, as though he had digestive issues (hence the need for appetite stimulants) and that the liver area was tight. I often associate the feeling of tightness in this area with suppressed anger. I knew that Cocoa had a need to be the leader in the house (he was the oldest cat) and also that he enjoyed peace and harmony. My client and I discussed this, and she revealed that Cocoa enjoyed sleeping in the same spot on her bed at night. She revealed that the "bully" cat had lately been running Cocoa off his spot and claiming it for himself! She said that she'd do anything to help Cocoa, so she told me she'd just have him on her bed at night and keep the other cats out. When she said that, I could feel Cocoa's body relax. It was at that point that the client gasped and said, "Cocoa just came out from under the bed and went over and started eating from his bowl!"

There are so many ways communicating with animals creates healing for those animals. Being in dialogue, not judging, being present, and being in gratitude radiates a healing energy that animals experience, appreciate, and benefit from. In my consultations with animals suffering from illness or injury, my first concern is that they've seen a veterinarian. I'll ask for a diagnosis and/or prognosis and also a list of prescribed drugs to get an idea of how to proceed.

My own health regimen includes medical doctors, naturopathy, chiropractic, and acupuncture. I manage my health through diet, fasting, supplementation, and exercise: yoga and hiking the mountains of the Blue Ridge. I stay pretty fit and healthy. Also included in this health regimen are therapies for emotional issues that have arisen over the years. The complications of life are such that I believe everyone needs counseling at one point with a trusted adviser. The perspective of another person is often crucial when facing life's dilemmas. Dialogue with someone trusted is a fabulous way to access and manage intense and unresolved energies in the body such as post-traumatic stress disorder (PTSD).

Traumatic events can be shoved into unconsciousness as a coping method. The memory of these events can emerge later in life and manifest as discomfort, illness, or depression—often giving rise to disease. As an example, I held a lot of unprocessed grief from my father's plane crash in my lungs and suffered many colds and bronchial issues throughout life. According to Chinese medicine, the lungs are associated with grief. Through therapy, I've been able to process that grief, and I no longer get colds at the drop of a hat. I have gotten great help from the Voice Dialogue process. It's not therapy but an excellent way to access emotional states too hidden or uncomfortable to deal with alone.

Similarly, an animal's health often improves after a session or two with an animal communicator. Here is a wonderful story submitted by one of my clients, Katie Donovan, who lives in Maine during the summer. She tells the story of her dog Bracken's illness resulting from bringing home a new pup, Farley.

Over the years, Diane Samsel has spoken to my dogs and me when I needed help, when there were misunderstandings, and even when they were lost and needed guidance to get home.

This story is about how Diane helped me to understand what happened to my beloved dog Bracken when I carefully planned to bring a new puppy into our pack. Bracken was then ten years old at the time.

The instant I arrived home after a week's absence with the new pup Fernley in tow, Bracken became extremely upset. He knew about Fernley's impending arrival, and through Diane, he had been trying to speak with the pup long distance. Bracken was very frustrated because Fernley did not respond to his visual images of animals such as deer, moose, and other creatures in his Maine domain. So, by the time Fernley and I arrived home, his short fuse had been lit and fueled by confusion and deep sadness. Why did we need this ignorant interloper in our pack? Fernley was just ten weeks old and a mere mite of a pup. There was no way she could receive the images being sent to her. Bracken felt rejected and powerless.

Following the introduction of Fernley, Bracken took himself upstairs in my cabin and lay under the eaves and would not come out. Period. For three days, he stayed there, in full retreat, mourning and growing increasingly lackluster before my alarmed eyes. He did not drink or eat or relieve himself—just lay on his bed looking more and more disconnected from life. Most alarming, his tongue began to swell, and he looked out from glassy eyes. Visits to the vet revealed no underlying health issues that could be addressed by their methods.

Enter Diane with her calm and knowing ways. She was able to convey Bracken's sadness to me. His sense of displacement, of being the aging wolf that is no longer top dog in the pack. Awareness of his pain made me feel sick at heart for and with him. Bracken and I are the same. I call us "HeMe." We have camped, canoed, hiked the hundred-mile wilderness, walked through Scotland, swum in lakes, mountain biked, and generally lived together as best friends since he was a pup.

Diane explained that Bracken experienced the new pup as an unneeded and rather useless creature. Bracken, who has a great vocabulary, called Fernley the "Silk Pillow." Fernley was so young and new to the world, and I don't think he understood that she might grow more useful in time. This was Bracken's first experience with puppyhood and the travails and joys inherent in the raising of a young dog.

With Diane assuring Bracken that his new purpose in life was to help train Fernley, and with Diane coaching me on how to ease his pain, he gradually came out from under the eaves and began the long, slow process of relating to a new pack dynamic. It was Diane's words between Bracken and me that I am convinced helped him to feel valued and understood and to give life another chance. Diane helped me to implement gentle action to restore his confidence and wellbeing. I will be forever grateful.

Now, two years later, Bracken is twelve and aging gracefully. He is a role model for me on how to stay in the game and to adjust to the challenges brought by changes within and without. I love that he and I have been together before . . . and may be again. He is the pup of my dreams. And he has accepted Fernley as part of his pack.

Fernley is now a joy in both our lives. She is titled in conformation and obedience and often leads the pack hunt for birds. Thankfully, she is affectionate and so respectful of her elder companion. Each day the three of us venture forth on outdoor adventures, appreciating our separate and unique instincts.

As two strong Irish Red and White Setters, Bracken and Fernley bring a liveliness and purpose to my life that cannot be described, only felt. It is a gift to drink in the energy and ways of animals, especially my animal companions. Thanks to Diane, I have a better glimpse into their hearts and minds and into their animal nature.

Communication is at the heart of healing. To know that our feelings about our hurts and pains can be shared with another brings comfort and a sense of belonging that goes a long way towards helping the body repair damage from life's ups and downs, disappointments, and triumphs.

TO CHARGE OR NOT TO CHARGE?

I encourage my students to charge for their services once they feel confident. A friend of mine, riffing on the laws of thermodynamics, told me that there was no transformation without an exchange of energy. When you give your work away, your talent will be consumed, and chances are you will feel depleted. This occurs because the other person brought nothing to the experience except the expectation that they'd be taken care of in the transaction. They had nothing at stake and so probably gained nothing—it's akin to free entertainment. If you set a price, your talents will be appreciated and you'll have something to show for your efforts.

The joy of doing this work often feels like reward enough. However, unless you are doing charity work, working for free is not advised. It's a good way to get burned out. I limit my free work to charity work; I give small, local four-hour workshops to raise money for animal causes. I take nothing from these workshops; the animal group takes 100 percent. I have helped raise as much as $800 in a four-hour workshop doing this. One therapy horse group raised $2,500 after expenses sponsoring a two-day workshop, but since it required my taking four days out of my workweek, I did get paid for it.

MISTAKES HAPPEN

It's okay to make mistakes when communicating with animals, and you can expect to make your fair share of mistakes when starting professionally. Here are some of the mistakes I have made:

a) Contacting the wrong animal. When this happens, ask if you're describing another animal in the house or maybe one belonging to a close friend/relative. Often other animals will "butt in" on a call.

b) Not getting anything at all. Admit there's no good connection and excuse yourself. This rarely happens to me after twenty years, but when it does, I am honest about it (and I never charge for my time).

c) Your client is totally unhappy with their appointment. You can sense when a client isn't enrolled in the information you're sharing with her. My rule of thumb is that the client is always right. I will refund money or not charge in the first place if my services are not appreciated. This happens now so infrequently that it's not a problem, but recently I did have an unhappy client (lost animal—I had initially found the dog but had tracked his spirit instead of focusing on where the body was located—a common error). She was upset that I hadn't cautioned her enough about the fact that her dog might be in spirit, and she was right. I had not followed my usual procedure for preparing my client. We actually argued in a polite way over payment. I didn't want to get paid; she wanted to pay me. So we compromised when I requested she donate the money to an animal rescue organization. I do this as a way of keeping myself honest.

In the early stages of my career, it stung to admit I was wrong, and to prevent any fudging, I just made my refund policy a way to maintain integrity and not give in to the desire to excuse my mistakes. As an aside, this client eventually called me back about another problem, and we had a very successful communication. She told me my integrity had impressed her, and she believed in my skills.

d) Forgetting an appointment. In the beginning of my practice, I had a hard time reconciling the timeless, spaceless psychic world with the world of concrete events and linear time. I would forget to check my calendar for appointments and just leave the house to shop or have lunch with a friend. Or I'd fall asleep or get busy with a project away from my office. This was early in my practice, and I was not balancing responsibility and working with the unknown very well. Here's a cute story sent to me from a client in New Jersey, Margaret Sharon, about her experience with my not being at the phone at the appointed hour:

The communication session I remember the best is the one that almost didn't happen. We had set an 8:00 p.m. appointment via phone call, and I told my horse Bud E. as I left the barn that Diane would be speaking to him later in the day. At the time of the appointment, I called and got no answer. Thinking my clock may have been early, I waited until 8:05 then called again and again. There was no answer. By 8:15, I had given up and said aloud, "Sorry, Bud—she's not answering the phone. Anything you can do?" Less than five minutes later, Diane called me. She'd explained that she had minor surgery earlier in the day and had dropped off to sleep early because of the anesthetic. The rest of the session was normal, and Bud E., who felt he had delivered Diane up, felt pretty smug about helping out!

PROTECTING YOURSELF WHEN DOING THIS WORK

Early in my career, I often attracted clients who were not in integrity. They might lie to me, refuse to pay me, or even ask my help in doing something illegal and harmful to an animal.

I learned that it took courage to stand up for animals in a communication session. If someone was not telling me the truth and the animal was, I stood with the animal. In one session held at a convention site back in the day when I was building my practice, a beautiful golden retriever told my client that her husband was hurting their children. I communicated this to the client, and she abruptly walked away from the session. It was clear from her reaction that she knew this to be true.

At another session, I received a phone call from a man who lived in New Jersey. He wanted to know if I could help him train his two Labrador retrievers to do something that was illegal and morally reprehensible. I told him no and hung up. The man had given me an address and phone number (required for an appointment), and I took it to the police and reported him. They got back to me later to report that they had called the police in the New Jersey town the man lived in. That police department sent two officers to the man's house and talked with him about the incident. The man denied the charges and the police left. What did that accomplish? I don't know. But I do know that he knows there is a report of his behavior on file, and maybe he'll think twice about his plans for his dogs.

TOOLS AND
TECHNIQUES

*A*ll professionals have a set of tools, methods, or techniques they use to help them be more effective in their field. Here, in no particular order, I'm going to share with you some of mine that I have found useful in my practice over the past twenty years. No doubt as you get deeper into your practice you will develop some of your own, and I hope you too will share your methods with others

VOICE DIALOGUE AND BONDING PATTERNS WITH ANIMALS

I mentioned Voice Dialogue in an earlier section, but I've found the technique so useful, particularly with respect to the bonds we form with animals, that I think it is worth mentioning again and providing a little more detail.

As for bonds, in my experience the bonds we form with family, friends, loved ones, and animals can be positive or negative. They can and do flip from one to the other in predictable patterned ways. It is a lifetime's work to stand between and acknowledge both our negative and positive feelings for and about one another. I was fortunate in that, early in my career, I was able to work with Dr. Susan McClure in Charleston, SC. From Dr. McClure, I learned about the work of doctors Hal and Sidra Stone, who as you'll recall, developed a facilitation technique in the early 1970s called Voice Dialogue. Using that technique, I've been able to successfully identify and address negative bonds between my human and animal clients.

Essentially, when my clients have troubling relationships with animals, I often have the client talk to me as if they are the animal that is creating problems—to assume that animal's personality and pretend they are the animal. I have the client get into another chair in the room and to the best of their ability talk as if their animal were talking with me. Then I have a conversation with the animal through the human caregiver. This helps my human client view the situation from the animal's perspective. It also helps the human client liberate her authentic self with which to view her own behavior, and then with that added clarity, work with me to find a path to resolution.

A client of mine had a difficult time housebreaking her boxer puppy. She experienced the pup as being defiant, and she had gotten into an uncomfortable bond with him, blaming him for his behavior and expressing her frustration and anger. She thought my technique of having her talk to me as her pup was odd, but she was a good sport. Right away, after speaking with me as her dog, she captured for herself the dog's frustration at not understanding what was required of him. Assuming the dog's perspective, she was able to appreciate how unreasonable she was being and how she was letting her feelings sabotage the patience needed for the task of potty training.

She saw that in her efforts to train, she was projecting the obstinate daughter who lived inside of her, the one who did not want to follow orders. She confessed that she had quite a rebellious streak as a young child that she had to disown. The little boxer was receiving such mixed messages simply because his person was guiding his training from the perspective of a five-year-old in full rebellion.

Most healthy animals want to serve and will quickly pick up our desires and do their best to fulfill them. However, if we humans are conflicted about what we want, the animal will not get the correct signals. My client was able to shift her perspective on the entire training process once she felt compassion for her inner rebel. Her young dog no longer had to carry that archetype and was free to be himself. He was quite eager to please it turned out.

I've used this process with a number of my clients with great success. I'll give my synopsis here of the concepts behind it, but for a more thorough understanding, I suggest reading *Embracing Our Selves: The Voice Dialogue Manual*, written by the Stones.[7]

The Voice Dialogue theory posits that our personalities are composed of many sub-personalities that are governed by an "operating ego." The operating ego functions much like the processor in a computer, calling forth a sub-personality when the function of that personality is needed. These sub-personalities are called "selves" and each of us carries within us many selves. Each of these selves has a unique perspective from which it sees the world.

How and when we call up a particular "self" is usually situationally dependent. Unfortunately, we don't always make the best choices when we call up a particular aspect of our personality. Voice Dialogue helps us identify when our responses, i.e., the personality we choose to address a particular situation, are out of step with our goals for that encounter. In the case above, the client had disowned her youthful and rebellious self and was projecting it onto her puppy. Voice Dialogue helped broaden her awareness of the impacts of her behavior.

Voice Dialogue is very potent stuff. There are tons of material available from reliable, reputable sources online related to the training and use of Voice Dialogue. You should be aware that, in this business, you are often going to be dealing with behavioral issues of some kind. If you want to maximize your utility to your clients, I highly recommend becoming at least familiar with Voice Dialogue.

ASTROLOGY AND ANIMAL COMMUNICATION

The intuitive skills of the animal communicator bring client and their animal companions closer together by bridging the language gap; the results are often astounding and always rewarding. But a problem exists in that important issues sometimes do not get addressed because the animal may not have the "words" or images to convey the problem. Often stoic animals will go to great lengths to hide their troubles. Accessing and discussing these unexpressed issues hold enormous healing potential, but the challenge is *how* to access these hidden problems.

I recently had one such session. The dog, Monty, I was communicating with could only state that he was confused, and I could feel that he was depressed. Monty's person, a new client, wasn't offering any suggestions as she was trying to stay neutral in order to test the validity of the communication. This "testing and withholding" happens frequently with first-time clients, and who can blame them! A good dose of healthy skepticism often provides the foundation of a great client relationship while trust is being established.

I was able to get to the heart of Monty's problem even though Monty was not able to express it himself and his guardian was being "guarded." I have been a professional astrologer for as long as I've been an animal communicator. A number of years ago, I began to combine the two disciplines. This practice began as a simple experiment when I cast an astrology chart for an animal communication session just to see what the chart might say about the session. I was astounded by how closely the symbols in the chart matched up to what was being communicated in the session!

I used my astrological program on my computer to draw up the chart for Monty's consultation. Although the first thing I picked up intuitively with Monty involved relationship tensions, the chart I had drawn for the session clearly showed that relationships indeed were under extreme stress. I mentioned this to Monty's person, and only then did she reveal that she had recently broken up with her partner. Both partners were now sharing Monty, and they were both carrying a lot of anger for the other. This was the source of Monty's depression. His loyalties were torn. My client and I discussed things she could do to help Monty adjust, and weeks later, she reported back that he had become a happy dog once again.

It took just a few measurements in this consultation chart to appreciate Monty's difficulties. The standouts involved the planet Venus, which represents relationship, in a difficult alignment with the planet Mars, which represents aggression and anger among other things. There were other symbols that backed up the information coming from Monty and his client, but the big issue was right there in the "angry relationship" issue that stood out in the consultation chart.

An astrological chart is easy to construct for an appointment. Astrolabe offers a good, free astrology chart: http://alabe.com/freechart/[8]. Basic astrology programs for the computer can also be inexpensive and easy to use. I use Io Edition—a very user-friendly program for Mac computers sold by Time Cycles Research, https://timecycles.com/.[9] By learning a few rules, using this tool can enhance your practice greatly.

The astrological chart is divided into twelve Houses of 30 degrees each based on the longitude and latitude of the location for which it is cast (such as the location of someone's birth). Figure 2 is an example of a blank wheel that shows the House divisions but not planets or aspects. Begin reading this chart from House 1, which is the Ascendant. Imagine the chart as a compass turned upside down with the Earth at the center (read counterclockwise beginning on the far left side): The easternmost direction (the left side) represents the Ascendant or First House. In the northernmost direction lies the IC (Imum Coeli—bottom of the sky) or Fourth House. The westernmost direction holds the Descendant or Seventh House, and finally, in the southernmost direction, we place the MC, Midheaven (Medium Coeli—top of the chart) or Tenth House (see figure 2).

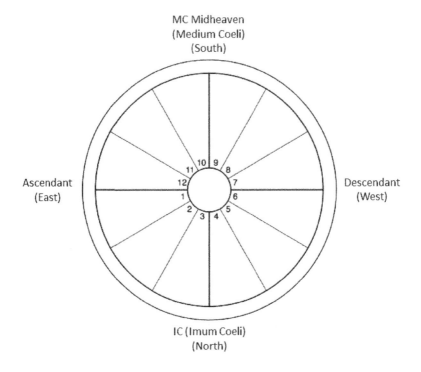

Figure 2 - Astrological Chart House Divisions

When the chart is cast, each House will fall in general alignment with one or two of the twelve signs of the zodiac. The zodiac is fixed in space. With the Earth at the center of this chart, it is easy to see that as the Earth rotates, the spokes of the chart (from the perspective of a fixed point on Earth) align with a new sign every two hours (the Earth's twenty-four hour period of revolution divided by the twelve zodiac signs). At the moment for which the chart is cast, the sign (and degree) of the zodiac rising in the east becomes the chart's rising sign.

A populated astrological chart, usually referred to as a horoscope during consultations, contains a number of symbols, including those for planets, the signs of the zodiac, and symbols indicating various relationships, which are called aspects. Think of an astrological chart as a play with the planets representing the actors, the signs representing the script, and the Houses representing the stage upon which the action unfolds. When I began my practice, I found this classic analogy very helpful when thinking about the story embedded in a chart. Let's start with the actors.

THE PLANETS

There are ten planets in the zodiac (the Sun and the Moon are included; the Earth in this count is excluded). The planets each have their own orbit and are in constant motion in the sky. Each individual astrological chart will have the planets fall in the different Houses depending on the place, date, and time for which the chart is cast. The two most important planets are the Sun (the energy we burn to get our needs met) and the Moon (our reigning need).

Here is a table showing the planets, their symbols, and their various representations. Note that this is not an exhaustive list of all heavenly bodies and symbols used in astrology, but it is sufficient for our purposes:

Planet	Symbol	Representation
Sun	☉	Ego, the fuel you burn to meet your needs
Moon	☽	The reigning need in life
Mercury	☿	Communication and mindset
Venus	♀	Beauty, relationship, and values
Mars	♂	Action and leadership
Jupiter	♃	Rewards and opportunities, enthusiasm
Saturn	♄	Lessons and constraints
Uranus	♅	Breakdowns and breakthroughs—bringing insight
Neptune	♆	Creativity and spirituality as well as deception and confusion
Pluto	♇	Transformation, perspective, power, sex, and death (as in the death of a cherished ideal)

Table 1 - The Planets and their Representations

THE SIGNS

The signs of the zodiac carry meaning and are the script of the play that is created by the astrological chart.

There are twelve signs, each of which will be in general alignment with one of the Houses when the chart is cast. Each sign is ruled by a planet. Some of the signs are ruled by the same planet. For instance, Gemini and Virgo are both ruled by Mercury. Here is the breakdown:

Sign	Symbol	Keywords	Planetary Ruler
Aries	♈	Initiates, leadership	Mars
Taurus	♉	Pleasure, beauty, and art	Venus
Gemini	♊	Communication, seeking diversity	Mercury
Cancer	♋	Emotional bonding, comfort, home, and mother	Moon
Leo	♌	Self-expression and creativity	Sun
Virgo	♍	Productive and discerning	Mercury
Libra	♎	Relationship, balance, and esthetics	Venus
Scorpio	♏	Perspective, empowerment, transformation	Pluto
Sagittarius	♐	Higher learning, law and beliefs, marketing, international travel	Jupiter
Capricorn	♑	Structure, form, and authority, practicality, and father	Saturn
Aquarius	♒	Friends, community, helping others	Uranus
Pisces	♓	Imagination, idealization, and surrender	Neptune

Table 2 - Signs, Symbols, Keywords, and Planetary Rulers

Each House will carry one or sometimes two (termed intercepted) signs. Remember, the signs are fixed in space, while the House alignments—the spokes on the chart—are fixed to the Earth relative to the specific location for which the astrological chart is cast. Consequently, as mentioned, the astrological sign on the cusp of each House shifts to a new House roughly every two hours as the

Earth turns during the course of the day. For instance, notice that at time "X" in the following figure, Aries is on the Ascendant at the cusp of the First House, but two hours later the heavens have turned (relative to the Earth) so that Taurus is on the Ascendant.

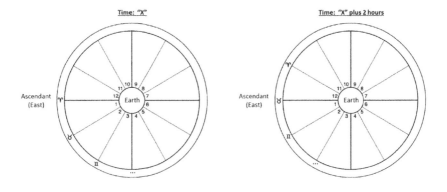

Figure 3 – Rotation of the Signs in the Sky Relative to a Fixed Point on Earth

ASPECTS

Planets form geometric relationships with each other, the Ascendant and the Midheaven. These relationships, called Aspects, develop as the planets move in their orbits. As an example, the Moon's orbit will take it around the Earth approximately every twenty-eight days. The Moon will make many different angular alignments, or aspects, with the other planets during this period. During that orbit, it will conjoin the Sun once (at the New Moon) and oppose the Sun once (at the Full Moon) and so on. This is referred to as a lunar cycle.

The primary (referred to as Ptolemaic) aspects are the Conjunction, Opposition, Trine, Square and Sextile. These are the most important and usually the strongest aspects between planets. The horoscope represents a 360-degree circle. The Opposition aspect is 180 degrees (that is, two planets of concern are 180 degrees apart, directly opposite from one another on the chart). The Trine is 120 degrees, the Square is 90 degrees, and the Sextile is 60 degrees.

Here is a breakdown of the aspects, their symbols, and the major dynamics expressed by them:

Aspect	Symbol	Dynamic
Conjunction	☌	Two planets are together and compete for expression.
Square	☐	Two planets form a 90-degree angle to one another; there's usually tension that needs to be resolved by turning a corner.
Opposition	☍	Two planets are separated by 180 degrees and need to be aware of one another.
Trine	△	Two planets form a 120-degree angle and the energy flows easily between them.
Sextile	✶	Two planets are 60 degrees apart and communicate easily with one another.

Table 3 - Aspects

The following chart is a summary of all the symbols we've discussed. I think you'll find it useful for quick reference in the next section where we begin to put the story together:

Signs		Planets		Aspects	
Aries	♈	Sun	☉	Conjunction	☌
Taurus	♉	Moon	☽	Square	☐
Gemini	♊	Mercury	☿	Opposition	☍
Cancer	♋	Venus	♀	Trine	△
Leo	♌	Mars	♂	Sextile	✶
Virgo	♍	Jupiter	♃		
Libra	♎	Saturn	♄		
Scorpio	♏	Uranus	♅		
Sagittarius	♐	Neptune	♆		
Capricorn	♑	Pluto	♇		
Aquarius	♒				
Pisces	♓				

Table 4 - Consolidated Table of Signs, Planets, and Aspects

PUTTING THE STORY TOGETHER

THE HOUSES

As mentioned, the horoscope is divided into twelve parts called the astrological Houses. The Houses provide the stage upon which the action takes place. Each House carries a meaning. House 1, the Ascendant, begins at the left side, midway between the top and bottom. The Houses circle the chart counterclockwise and, when the chart is cast, each House has the symbol of one of the signs of the zodiac at its beginning. Here are some basic themes of each House:

House	Theme
First	The persona—Personality: Who I am
Second	Value system—Self-worth: What I own and trust
Third	Mindset—Communications: What and how I communicate
Fourth	Core emotions—Parent: Comfort and belonging, home, how I feel
Fifth	Love expressed—Creativity: How I express
Sixth	Productivity—Cooperation: How I work
Seventh	Relationships—Partnerships: My relationships
Eighth	The values of others—Other's resources: How I trust others
Ninth	Belief system—The story of life: What I stand for
Tenth	Status in the community—Parent: My profession, how I manage my life
Eleventh	Community—Those I associate with: How I receive love and appreciation
Twelfth	Surrender—Letting go and preparing for the next cycle: How I am able to move on in life

Table 5 - The Houses and their Themes

The astrological chart represents a snapshot of the Earth and its relationship to the planets and stars at any given moment of the day. Remember to start reading the chart from the middle of the left side (east—called the Ascendant or the Rising Sign) and read counterclockwise. Recall that the Ascendant is the point on a horoscope where the Sun rises in the morning and is said to be the cusp (beginning) of the First House. At the bottom (or north) part of the chart is the cusp of the Fourth House, known as the IC (Imum Coeli). On the right (west) is the cusp of the Seventh House and on top (south) is the cusp of the Midheaven or Tenth

House. We will rarely use these terms here, but you will often see them elsewhere in most astrological chart descriptions.

HOUSE RULERSHIPS

Recall that each sign is "ruled" by a planet (see the Signs section above for a list of signs and their rulers). Planetary rulerships are key to the process of determining the importance of planetary placements in the chart. Recall also that each House of a horoscope has a sign associated with the portion of the zodiac that lies at the House's cusp. The planet that rules the sign on the cusp also rules the House and describes issues associated with that House. However, it is possible, as you'll see, that planets within a House may fall under the next sign. In that case, the planetary ruler of that sign rules them.

For instance, you'll see below in the horoscope of my cat Buster that the planet Jupiter rules the Ascendant of the chart, so the placement of Jupiter is critical. The ruler of the Ascendant is said to rule the chart, therefore Jupiter rules the chart. Jupiter is placed in the Second House of Buster's horoscope and is conjunct (that is, forms a Conjunction with) Neptune. This combination suggests a high degree of spiritual importance for the individual. Buster radiated a beautiful spirit to all who met him.

Let's take a closer look.

MEET BUSTER

Below is an example of the astrological chart of my Maine Coon cat, Buster. The triangle with all the symbols and planet glyphs below the chart shows all of the aspects made by the planets shown in the chart. Most of us do not know the birth time of our animals, but since Buster and I had worked together while he went through his reincarnation experience, I knew who his breeder was. After the dream where he told me he was being born,

I awoke and noted the time. When I called the breeder at 9 a.m., she told me she had been up all night birthing the new litter! From the dream and what the breeder mentioned, I was able to set a time of birth for Buster.

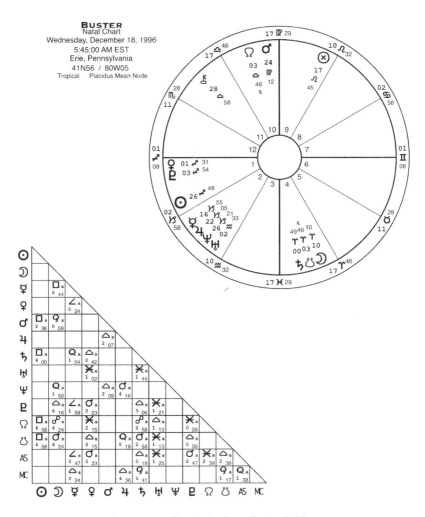

Figure 4 – Buster's Astrological Chart

When the chart was cast, the Fourth House was positioned so that it spanned the end of Pisces (late Pisces at the cusp) and the beginning of Aries. You can see that the Fourth House runs from 17 degrees Pisces through 17 degrees Aries. The symbols next to the Moon show that the Moon falls at "10 ♈"—that is, roughly ten degrees into the sign of Aries. If you interpreted Buster's chart, you would see that his Sun (the energy he burns to get his needs met) is in the sign Sagittarius on the Ascendant of the First House and his Moon (his reigning need in life) is in the sign Aries in the Fourth House.

From the previous tables we know the following:

Planet	Symbol	Representation
Sun	☉	Ego, the fuel you burn to meet your needs
Moon	☽	The reigning need in life
Mars	♂	Action and leadership
Jupiter	♃	Rewards and opportunities, enthusiasm
Neptune	♆	Creativity and spirituality as well as deception and confusion

Sign	Symbol	Keywords	Planetary Ruler
Aries	♈	Initiates, leads	Mars
Sagittarius	♐	Higher learning, law and beliefs, marketing, international travel	Jupiter

The Sun in the First House (persona) under Sagittarius (ruled by Jupiter) describes Buster's enthusiasm. His Sun receives a square from Saturn, which suggests his exuberance needs restraint and control. He's the good-natured lawmaker, greeting everyone with gusto while firmly enforcing the rules.

Buster's Moon, in Aries, lies in the Fourth House (home) and describes his reigning need to be number one around the house. We call Buster "the sheriff" because he's very bossy and likes us to follow the rules (breakfast at 7:30!). But he's also nice because we see the planet Venus (relationship) there on his Ascendant (his personal ego projection). He has a social personality (Venus) and is friends (Venus) with everyone! Let's use Buster's chart as an example of the analogy of the horoscope as a play. You see that since Buster's Sun falls in his First House in Sagittarius, his life drama's script has him expressing a strong belief in himself as a leader among cats and humans, with his Moon in Aries in the Fourth House representing his reigning need to be number one.

CONSTRUCTION OF A CONSULTATION CHART: TURNING THE CHART

To prepare for a consultation, I construct a chart for the moment the session begins (as I mentioned, I use a computer program to do this). This is called a Consultation Chart. To assess the qualities of my animal client, I "turn the chart." I use the cusp of the Sixth House in the consultation chart as the Ascendant of the chart I'll be using for the animal client. The Sixth House represents many things, and I use it for the animals that are important to us.

I believe our animal friends come into our lives to be of service to us and to help us to improve. These are matters of the Sixth House. "Turning a chart" refers to a simple technique that allows you to place the Ascendant of the consultation chart on the cusp of any of the twelve Houses of that chart—and thereby derive a new chart from the original chart. When a client calls me, I cast a consultation chart for that moment using my location. I use the Ascendant to tell me about my human client—what his/her issues and needs might be. I use the Sixth House to give me information about my animal client.

With the turned chart's Sixth House now the Ascendant of the animal's part of the chart, I can construct an entirely new chart. When the consultation chart's Sixth House becomes my animal client's First House, it follows that the Seventh House becomes the animal client's Second House and so on. As you continue counterclockwise around the chart, the turned chart gives you a totally new chart that describes your animal client's condition accurately.

As an example of how this works, let's look at my astrological chart and the Sixth House of that chart to see what role my animals play in my life:

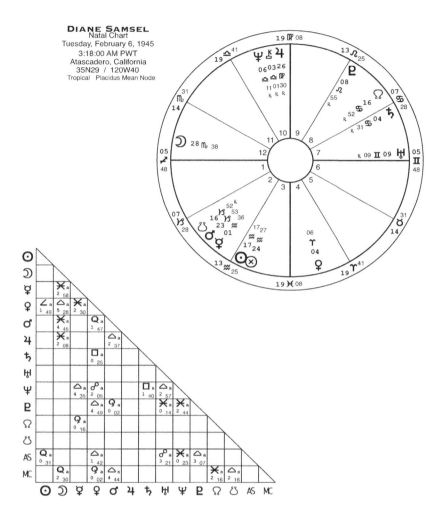

Figure 5 - Diane's Astrological Chart

You can see that Taurus is the sign on the cusp of my Sixth House. To find my cat Buster's chart from my chart, I would turn my chart's Ascendant to my Sixth House, and that would become Buster's chart's Ascendant. Notice that the Taurus rising in the turned chart is echoed in Buster's birth chart, which has Venus conjunct the Ascendant. Venus rules Taurus. The Moon in my chart lands in the Seventh House of the turned chart, which tells me how my reining need (Moon) affects Buster. My Moon falls into his Seventh House of relationship and is in Scorpio, so our relationship is important to the healing work I do. In many ways, Buster is an ambassador for emotional healing in relationships. He would sit on my desk during consultations and help my animal clients as I worked with them.

USING "CHART TURNING" FOR CONSULTATIONS

Constructing a chart for a consultation leads to similar insights into the relationship between your client and her animal companion. The Ascendant will represent the client, and the Sixth House will represent the client's animal companion. To focus on the animal, I begin by casting a consultation chart for the time of the appointment and use the Sixth House as the Ascendant for the animal I'll be working with in the session. To illustrate how this works, here is a chart for a consultation that began at 5:30 p.m. on February 11, 2010:

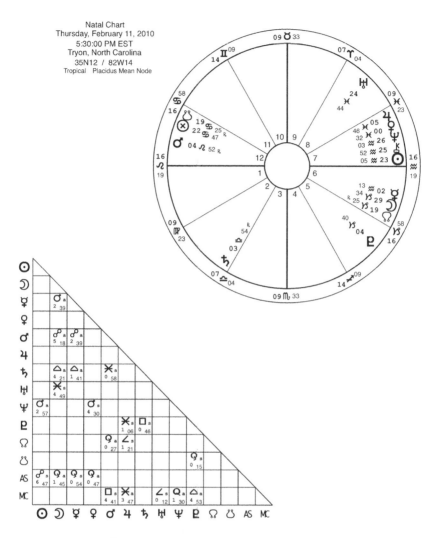

Figure 6 - Sample Consultation Chart

Here are the steps to use the chart:

1. Determine the Ascendant for the human client. The human client's Ascendant is always on the cusp of the chart's First House. Leo is the sign on the Ascendant. Leo is ruled by the Sun, and the Sun falls

in the Seventh House (relationship). Notice in the aspect grid that the planet Neptune is conjunct the Sun. That can suggest confusion.

2. Determine the Ascendant of the turned chart representing the animal client. It falls on the cusp of the consultation chart's Sixth House. Capricorn is on the cusp of the Sixth House, and Capricorn is ruled by Saturn. The Sixth House holds the Moon conjunct Mercury. The Sun of the turned chart falls in the Second House of self-worth.

3. Consider the planetary relationships. As mentioned, the Sun of the consultation chart is in the Seventh House, representing relationship, and it conjoins Neptune. Sun is energy, and Neptune can suggest confusion, so the client might be losing energy over a confusing situation with her cat.

The Sixth House, representing the cat's First House, has Capricorn (practicality) on the cusp and holds the Moon. In this chart, Pluto squares Saturn, and Pluto rules the Fourth House (home). Pluto represents transformation, and Saturn represents constraints. This would suggest that an issue with home might be of great concern to the cat. The Capricorn and Moon energy suggest the cat would regard the problem with an emotionally practical approach.

The consultation turned out to be about the client's unsettled living conditions and her fear and confusion over what to do with her cat. The cat was, indeed, very practical about their situation. He suggested moving to her mother's house until my client could get her life back on track. And that's what my human client agreed to do! After that, the problem resolved itself.

I also use this method to help people find their lost animals. I construct the chart for the time the consultation begins using my location. I look to the Sixth House of this chart, which represents the animal, and then I look for the House in which the ruler of the Sixth House resides. (Start counting at the Sixth House! Remember, this is a turned chart and is derived from the consultation chart, so House Six will become the Ascendant or "House One" of the lost animal).

Recently a long-term client called with a lost cat, and I didn't have time to fit her into my schedule. Since I had my computer open, I first located where the ruler of the Sixth House (representing the lost cat) was at that moment (it resided in the turned chart's Eighth House—remember, start at House One of the turned chart and count eight Houses counterclockwise to arrive at the "turned" Eighth House). I suggested she look near garbage or refuse piles—Eighth House (as you'll see below) rules garbage! The next day, she contacted me to say they had found the kitty by the garbage cans outside. I use my intuitive skills in conjunction with astrology, so while talking with this client, the cat was showing me garbage cans.

The chart helped nail it!

I have a specialized list I keep handy of places that each House represents—see below. I use it to quickly identify locations suggested by a chart for a lost animal. If the ruler of the Sixth House is in the derived:

House	Location
First	Abandoned place
Second	Garden areas, farm, or woodlands
Third	Neighborhoods, freeway, schoolyard, concrete watercourse
Fourth	Barn, basement, cul-de-sac, near home, body of water
Fifth	Playground, racetrack, feral cat colony, park, golf course
Sixth	Closet, garage, storage place, kennel
Seventh	Someone else's home (often animal is being cared for by someone)
Eighth	Deep pit, cave, cemetery, trash dump, junkyard, landfill
Ninth	Attic, church, college, distant location, place with horses
Tenth	Construction site, business site, office space, top of something (rafters, attics, and trees)
Eleventh	Airport, club room, meeting room, vortex, mineral spring
Twelfth	Bar, churchyard, prison, institution, deep hiding place where they feel safe

Table 6 – Possible Lost Animal Locations Based on the Derived Location of the Ruler of the Sixth House

During another recent session, I visited with Ringo, a dog I have talked with several times. I could tell Ringo was anxious and that he felt a strong need to give love to his person. I had the consultation chart in front of me, and my eye went immediately to the Moon (home) conjoined Uranus (changes). I said to my human client, "Ringo seems to be anxious about changes in the home."

My client was astounded! Her partner, and Ringo's other parent, had suddenly moved out.

Astrology can be a complex discipline that takes years to master. But I've found that by learning a few symbols and applying this system, it offers an easy to use technology for the animal communicator.

THE SIX HEALTH DILEMMAS

Working as an astrologer helped me realize that my animal clients' health issues could be categorized into six major sectors based on the twelve Houses of the astrological chart. I almost never have an astrological birth chart of an animal in front of me when I work, but I know enough about life stresses that may lead to disease. The consultation chart I have for each communication session will suggest areas of health concerns to explore. The dyad created by the opposing Houses creates a need for awareness. If there is stress in one House, it can affect the opposite House.

Healthy individuals, both human and non-human, are:

1. Able to maintain routine bodily maintenance, good boundaries, and openness to others. Able to create partnerships and share with others. These are First and Seventh House issues.

2. Filled with a sense of self-worth and respect for others. Able to trust themselves and others. These are Second and Eighth House issues.

3. Able to communicate needs and make sense out of what is communicated by others. They know when information received is true and can believe

in themselves and others. These are Third and Ninth House issues.

4. Able to handle disappointment and are able to feel they belong to a family where they receive emotional validation and also feel that they can make a difference in the world. These are Fourth and Tenth House issues.

5. Able to give and receive love and to express themselves in a creative way. They can play, take risks, and be a beloved member of the larger community. These are Fifth and Eleventh House issues.

6. Productive, cooperative and compassionate, and able to surrender the self to the needs of others when necessary. Discernment creates healthy habits and an ability to feel okay with the universe. Able to let go of old business when necessary. These are Sixth and Twelfth House issues.

Life, being complex, often makes it difficult to pursue a balanced ideal of self-care. When circumstances put an animal out of balance in any of the above areas of life, predictable health issues may arise. I call these the health dilemmas and have condensed them into a list of six in close correlation with the above House-related health attributes. Here is my list:

1. **Me vs. You:** Animals that are either defensive or codependent. Possible health problems could affect the head or the kidney area. These animals need to learn healthy body boundary setting skills.

2. **Mine vs. Yours:** Animals that have self-worth issues or can be controlling and manipulative in relationships. Possible health problems might involve the

neck area and/or the genitals. These animals need to identify what they value and learn to respect the values of others. They need to learn to trust themselves and set boundaries in situations of low trust without being manipulative.

3. **My thoughts vs. Your thoughts:** Animals with learning difficulties. These problems can arise when early training is neglected, harsh, or inappropriate, leaving the animal with unfinished business around learning. The animal may have difficulty paying attention and following simple requests. These animals may also have a hard time processing information because they do not believe in themselves and their abilities.

Possible health problems could affect the lungs and digestive systems. These animals need to develop skills that enable them to make sense of what is to be learned from day-to-day experiences. They need to learn to listen carefully to others and trust the information they're receiving. They need to know that what they're communicating is being respected.

4. **At home vs. Out in the world:** Animals that have unresolved emotional issues affecting their ability to get their needs met or animals that exhibit difficulties with issues of maturity and ability to achieve. Possible health problems would involve the stomach and skeletal system.

These animals need to learn emotional grounding and/or skills that enable them to express authority. They need to feel like they belong and can make a difference.

5. **Love given vs. Love received:** Animals that have difficulties giving or receiving appreciation, love, and attention stemming from unfinished business from adolescence. They often don't feel lovable or have a difficult time expressing love. Possible health problems might involve the heart and the circulatory system.

    These animals need help learning to be self-expressed and to take healthy risks. They often need to learn to be open to the good that comes to them in the form of affection and appreciation from friends and others in their community.

6. **Productivity vs. Surrender:** Animals that have problems with productivity, cooperation, and duty that stem from not knowing the right time to surrender. They often feel victimized as a defense or are workaholics in order to please their companions/trainers. They may have issues that arise from improper training or no training at all. Possible health problems would involve the bowels, feet, and hard-to-diagnose illnesses.

    These animals need to limit their efforts, and learn how to pace their activities and when to rest. They need to develop compassion for themselves and others, and above all, how to let go.

For more information on House-related health issues, I highly recommend Michael Munkasey's great sourcebook: *The Astrological Thesaurus - Book 1: House Keywords*.[10] It is another much-used book within reach of my desk. I suggest having this book in your reference library for a more complete list of health issues as they pertain to the astrological Houses.

ENERGY CLEANSING

Earlier, while discussing a "not so typical" session with my client Linda and her deer family, I mentioned also addressing some of Linda's horse's exaggerated fear of a door (once visited by a snake) and the arena it led to. I said that I had done a little energy work to clear the arena of the heavy energy that had filled it. To clear the arena, I used a simple clearing exercise I've been doing for decades. Here's how that works:

> Meditate and center yourself then imagine a sheet of white light stretched out a few feet beneath the ground of the area to be cleared. Imagine an angel on each corner slowly lifting the sheet of white light until it's well off the ground. Have the angels bring together the corners, tie them together with a ribbon of your favorite color, and send the sheet and any dark energy off into space to be recycled. You may find resistance during this exercise as you capture heavy energies in the process. Stay with the process, and it will eventually lift off! This clearing can be done as frequently as needed.

As horses and their riders train, emotions of frustration, disappointment, anger, even boredom—and, of course, the fear of snakes—may arise from both rider and horse. These feelings represent a natural process during any practice or training session. The energy from these emotions can accumulate into a heavy energy, and like any dust or debris, requires a cleansing. All of us have at one time walked into a room and felt a negative "vibe." When humans interact intensely and matters don't get resolved, energy can stay a bit stuck. Some type of cleansing is in order, and using the sheet of white light is one of my favorites.

SPIRITUALITY, LIFE HACKS, AND OBSERVATIONS ON LIFE, THE UNIVERSE, AND EVERYTHING

I'm often invited to teach animal communication and have done so at seminars across the country. At the end of each session, I open the floor to questions from the audience. As you can imagine, this generally turns into a lively encounter covering a wide range of topics. And, of course, there are always the impromptu "meetings after the meeting" that occur at mealtimes. The following stories, observations, and tips are intended to respond to those questions, comments, or concerns that come up most often during my seminars.

THE BODY AS A RECEPTOR

I teach that the body is the primary receptor of information in animal communication, and I'm often asked if I can provide an example of reception beyond the usual five senses that would be recognized by scientists. And my answer is, "Of course I can!"

One very simple example concerns the discovery of magnetite in animals. Birds have magnetite in their brains that help them sense the Earth's magnetic field, an ability they use to navigate along their migration routes. Honeybees have magnetite (how *do* they find their hives after all that wandering around?). And, yes, cats use their bodies to navigate Earth's magnetic field too. Recent research discovered that there are receptors in cats' ankles that are sensitive to these energies.

Humans have magnetite in their pineal gland, but the jury is still out whether it helps us navigate. That said, several experiments have shown a measurable, repeatable brain wave shift when an external electric field is altered. Theories abound that electromagnetic navigation is a sense we evolved with but have since deemphasized as we developed more precise methods. My personal opinion is that we can and do take advantage of the Earth's magnetic field. If you have a friend who gets lost in a grocery store, that person probably has very little magnetite. I, on the other hand, can be set down anywhere on the globe and could probably find my way around. I'm guessing I have lots of magnetite. There are fascinating scientific as well as lay articles on this subject; just Google "animals and navigation." Or, if you're a science nerd like me, Google "scientific papers on animals and navigation."

DEATH, DYING, AND REINCARNATION

When the time comes in our animal's life to consider letting our cherished friend pass to spirit, enormous emotional issues can arise in the human guardian's heart. Humans often find letting their animals go to spirit an agonizing experience. Their animal friends cannot speak for themselves, and we humans can only watch in sadness as their bodies grow frail or as they withdraw in what we perceive as pain and suffering. Being humans, we cannot know what their experience might be, and we often project our emotions of doubt, fear, and especially guilt, onto the situation. Many clients express guilt at the end of their animal friend's life; they often feel that they haven't done enough or that they should have acted sooner to address health issues.

Humans often suffer from feelings of abandonment when death finally claims their loved one. In each of us, there is usually a deep core vulnerability that we share with our animal friend and often no one else. Our friend becomes our closest ally and a trusted family member, so losing that bond is often traumatic. This is true for a great many of my clients as well as myself. My bond with Buster was so strong that his loss shook me for weeks. This level of loss is often experienced as having "a hole in the heart." When death claims an animal with whom we have a strong bond, there actually is a "hole" left where the bond breaks, and it can be physically painful. These are energetic holes, but in many cases, no less painful than a physical hurt.

When I first started working with animals, I feared death. I learned from family members that my paternal grandmother feared death, and I think I may have inherited the fear from her. My mother seemed to have no fear of death although she grieved harder than anyone I have ever met when death came to one of her loved ones. Death threatened to overwhelm my psyche. The trauma of my father's tragic death in a midair collision when I was fifteen wounded me for decades. Working with animals in spirit helped me overcome my fears.

Animals have told me that dying is easy. They live in the present, and their perception of life comes from a profound spiritual presence they experience in the moment. For most animals, the richness and power of living in the now gives their lives peace and meaning. I was told many years ago by an animal client that he saw life as a cycle. You breathe in you have a body; you breathe out you don't have a body. They don't ruminate on a future with no body or regret the past when their bodies felt free and unencumbered by pain and the afflictions of age. Most animals that live with us are well prepared for the transition to spirit when the time arrives.

I've helped many human clients prepare for the death of their animal friends. Issues of care and whether their animal wants help passing are top priorities in these conversations. Questions arise such as "Should I continue with the cancer treatment?" The answers to these and many other questions are as varied as the personalities involved. When Rusty (my sweet buff-colored tabby) was ready for transition at the age of twenty, he came to me and said he wanted a natural death. He was approaching kidney failure and didn't want me to continue with Sub-Q treatments, which I had been administering several times a week for a few years. I took him to the vet for one last visit, and the dire numbers that came up for his kidney when he had a blood draw confirmed what Rusty already knew. I asked him about euthanasia, and his answer was no. He told me I needed to know what death looked like and that he intended to walk me through it.

Rusty's decline left me conflicted and uncomfortable. It was clear he was suffering, and at the same time, he was instructing me that he was okay and able to handle the process. Animals are stoic so as not to attract predators and have mechanisms for detaching from their pain and discomfort. Human societies used to "harden" their babies to make them ignore pain and suffering. My German farmer ancestors produced family members who told us to toughen up, ignore tender feelings and get on with life.

I was nine years old and getting into the car with my dad when he slammed the door on his hand. He drove us home while holding his bleeding hand off to the side so I wouldn't see it. He never said a word, but I knew from the ashen color of his face and the sweat pouring off that something was horribly wrong. My beloved aunt Dorothy Tennessee Samsel, his older sister, had stage-four breast cancer and never said a word. She didn't treat it with anything stronger than Tylenol, and she died with a tumor the size of a golf ball, which she hid with bulky clothing. No one in the family knew she was suffering so much. This is the effect of being trained to ignore physical pain. For much of our species' history ignoring pain has been an essential survival tactic. And so it is in animals.

As I mentioned, Rusty was dying of kidney failure, a decline which I've been told by doctors is not painful. My mother died at age ninety-six of kidney failure resulting from years of cardiovascular issues. The doctors said if they were given a choice of which disease to die from, it would be kidney failure. It's painless. As

Rusty began his descent into death, he stopped eating. The next stage was walking. He walked around the house a lot. He told me he was "letting go of extra energy." A day or so later, I awoke one morning to find Rusty stretched out on the floor, breathing shallowly. I knew he was close to death. He told me he had been waiting for me to wake up so he could show me his death. I gathered him up in his favorite basket and sat with him as he began his final stages of dying. In the end, he began to experience agonal breathing (that's when the brain dies). I was incredibly alarmed because he was making very loud noises.

Rusty got my attention at that point and showed me he was no longer in his body. He said he had been out of his body for some time and was not experiencing anything physically at that point. His little body gave a few more final breaths, and he lay still in his basket. I was sobbing for the loss of my friend but spiritually comforted by Rusty's presence in spirit, which I could see clearly. I was experiencing the physical pain of having the bond to his body broken. I took the basket upstairs, picked flowers for an arrangement, lit a candle and had a proper viewing for him before we laid him to rest in our family pet cemetery outside my office downstairs. After the other cats in the house were able to pay their respects, and after Rusty had adjusted fully to being outside his body, we buried him. At the head of his grave is a little statue of Kwan Yin, the Chinese goddess of compassion.

OUR FEAR OF DEATH

At the heart of our human fear of death is the fear of abandonment. This fear of abandonment begins when we're so young that we usually don't recall the first time that terror struck our hearts. My earliest memory of that horrible feeling goes back to when I was four years old and we were living in Lubbock, Texas. Dad headed up the Texas Tech Army ROTC program, and we lived in an apartment complex filled with young families and a few retirees. Mom wanted more than anything to travel back to South Carolina for Christmas. I can only imagine how out of place she felt in the barren Texas panhandle after being raised in the lush landscape of South Carolina. Dad was at home with the fishing, hunting, and built-in fraternity of army mates. Mom just had us two kids and her deep longing for home and the comforts of a large, extended family.

Cotton was a big commodity for the Lubbock area, and in the fall, the cotton industry needed lots of extra people to grade cotton. Mom signed on to the job to raise cash to take us all home for the holiday. Her longing and choice to go to work for the first time ushered me into traumatic events that left me afraid of death and storms.

Mom wasn't the only mother to take on cotton grading to earn more cash. A number of her neighbors also took the job. The mothers found a daycare center, and all of the children were taken to this center early on the first morning of cotton grading. I have just vague memories of this part of the story.

After a few weeks, the mothers began to notice their children were getting hysterical every time there was a storm. Mom said as the first storm approached, I became hysterical and hid in the closet. Concerned, some of the mothers asked their children what was going on and were shocked by the answers. The daycare center was run by a Christian fundamentalist cult. The adults were teaching us that we were wicked and that God was going to get us. Thunder and lightning was His way of letting us know He was on to us.

At the apartment complex, the children too young for school—myself included, of course—ran around in a wild pack. Unsupervised and full of energy (and with no TV or media to distract us), we tested boundaries that our most mischievous and intelligent and pathological members could come up with to tempt us. I was one of the younger ones and a great follower. There was the caper where we stole wholesale packages of hard candy from a delivery truck parked out front of the complex, panel doors left temptingly wide open to the treasures within. I still remember the delicious taste of those ill-gotten goods, which we divided up judiciously afterward. To this day, I won't turn down a piece of fruit-flavored hard candy—the type that's clear, shaped like a tiny one-inch log. That's just one of the infractions we conjured up. There were others.

We knew we were doing wrong. But our tiny brains, not yet hardwired to consequences, were not so convinced we would be caught. However, after the cult got a hold of us, we all knew the jig was up, and now God was coming after us. We were busted, and all of us were going to hell.

The mothers rightfully yanked their little traumatized fledglings out of the jaws of hell and found a much more suitable daycare situation at a nearby army facility. It was so military. Chain-link fences, rooms painted khaki—a painted wainscot in gloss and the rest of the wall matt. To this day, that color scheme manages to depress me! The high windows were covered with roll shades of the same khaki brown. It was beige and as sterile as a place can possibly be. As an army institution, it was run on a strict schedule. We napped at a certain time, we played at a certain time, and we had story time. No avenging gods touched us.

I remember running to the end of the playground the first day of this incarceration, grabbing the chain-link with both my little fists and sobbing and screaming for my mother to come back and save me. Then we had to take a nap in that hideous beige room. I stretched out on my mat alongside my little partners in crime, feeling trapped, abandoned, and so very heartbroken. Thus was my phobia of both severe storms and abandonment born in my awareness.

I think we all have stories like this buried in our pasts. There's nothing quite like losing a beloved animal friend to trigger the strong emotions of loss and abandonment reminiscent of what a child experiences when they first feel their little hearts breaking. But the loss of a cherished friend can be managed constructively. Indeed, it can also be a joyous event, a celebration of a full and happy life. Two of my clients have shared stories that I think are particularly on point.

DEXTER'S PASSING

It was so hard to see him suffer. We wanted to do anything we could to keep him alive, heal him. Our consultation with you switched our focus from what we thought was best for him (ourselves) to what he wanted—transition. "It is a joyous occasion." We were ready to permit extensive surgery on him when your reading came, and he said, "No, no, no . . . don't do anything. My fight is over. . . . I am going along with what is right for me. . . . I am a cat and my life span is over. . . . It has been a wonderful life. I have been spoiled rotten. . . . If you wouldn't mind, let me go. . . . I am at peace."

He wanted to help us understand and accept. His telling us that he had a great life with us helped ease our pain—and knowing that he was not in pain was even better. It was fascinating that at the end he wanted us to realize that he was teaching us how to endure end-of-life situations for others, "This is a lesson you need to learn. I am happy to go. . . . I have been kept alive beyond my expiration date . . . learn to take care of others." He also said, "Do not look at the transition as a fearful event. It is a job I have to do, and I am looking forward to it because I will be back with my ancestors."

He was an indoor/outdoor cat and a great hunter. You told us that cats are "programmed to just walk away and die. They call a predator to kill very efficiently, saves all the trauma." That was hard to hear, but it sounded in our hearts to be so true with Dexter. We live in a forested area with lots of predators and considered allowing him to go outside. But you said that in the wild, an animal would call a predator and that a vet who euthanizes is just like

a predator that helps an animal go out quickly. That is exactly what we did the next day. You saying that "Dexter is packed and ready to go. He is not concerned about how it happens." was the touch of humor we all needed.
    Submitted by Kathleen Samalon

ABBEY'S RETURN

I met Diane Samsel many years ago when I had my first "heart" dog, Abbey [a miniature schnauzer]. *She* [Diane] *was helping with a fund-raiser for a local animal shelter. I was in pure awe with the experience of her communicating with Abbey. Diane shared with me what Abbey's favorite view was and described my front yard and deck like she had been there herself! From that moment on, I knew animal communication was real!*

Many years later, Abbey was diagnosed with kidney failure. I was feeding her home-cooked food because she was limited on what she could eat, and I was giving her subcutaneous fluids at home every day. I arranged a phone appointment/reading with Diane so that I could get some insight into how Abbey was feeling, and to hopefully make myself feel better about it all. Diane had no idea that Abbey was sick. Within minutes of our phone call, with Abbey lying at my side, she sat straight up, as if she was in a trance! She did not move the entire time of Diane communicating with her! Diane told me that Abbey was sick and that Abbey relayed to her that she knew I was doing everything I could to help her and that, although she didn't like getting the fluids in her back, she knew it would help her feel better and that we could have more time together. She said Abbey told her to tell me she liked the chicken and rice, but to please go back to the way I used to make it!!! (This was on point!!!).

I asked about how I would know when it was time to

let her go, and Abbey told her she would let me know. I then asked if she would want to come back to me someday, and the answer was yes, as a girl again.

After losing her, I went to an Animal Communication class with Diane Samsel and Barbara Rawson. It was a very touching experience. Diane told me that there was a spirit dog sitting on the floor next to me and described her to me. It was Abbey!

I was totally lost after losing her and wanted her back so bad. It took almost two years of searching for a minia-ture schnauzer puppy in the Southeast, via Google search, before I finally found a breeder. It was finally going to happen!

We brought Gabby home, and as soon as she walked in the door, she went straight into the kitchen to her bowls!!! She walked around the house like she knew where everything was! I had the strangest feeling come over me, and when she turned and looked at me, I saw Abbey's eyes looking back at me! I knew my baby girl was back home with me!!!!

I've always been a believer, but living it is so much sweeter!

Thank you so much, Diane, for your wonderful and blessed gift!!! You've helped my world be a happy and brighter place!!!

Submitted by Tammy Kizer of Edisto Beach, SC

WHAT DOESN'T KILL YOU MAKES YOU STRONG

People often ask me how I became so attuned to the energies around me. I tell them that it developed in part from my belief system, but that I also think it was fueled by some rather severe life experiences.

I believe we are all part of a divine energy that informs everything in the universe. My ability to talk with animals, plants, and even rocks comes from trusting the information that flows through this divine energy and into my awareness. As the Bible states, "In the beginning was the Word." I was always extremely sensitive and empathic. I picked up the emotions of the adults around me and processed them without any understanding of what was happening. Army people back then tended to drink and party a lot, and I was around inebriated and somewhat out-of-control adults often in my childhood. I grew insecure as I was exposed to this darker side of adulthood with no understanding of what I was sensing, and my senses grew sharper.

This was the path my abandonment took early on—I began not to trust adults. I trusted other senses that informed me that the world was a wondrous place and that animals were fully sentient beings that I trusted. I knew to avoid rattlesnakes, certain spiders, and any animal that showed aggression, but on the whole, I was responsive to the open hearts most creatures exhibited when feeling relaxed and safe.

I had learned so early to distrust humans, and it was the few people who came into my life and gave me unconditional love that saved my life. Those people included a beloved aunt and a few teachers and neighbors. It doesn't take much kindness to make a big difference in a child's life.

A retired couple lived at our apartment building in Lubbock. Their daughter had been an airline stewardess, and they had lost her in a plane crash. When I came along, they fell in love with me and took me under their wing. I was a pale, skinny, stressed little kid, and they were health food enthusiasts. They had the first vegetable juicer I would see, and they started juicing carrots for me to put color in my cheeks. I still remember the love, affection, and care they gave me. I was blessed with their attention at a time when my life seemed mired in chaos. It was care from people like this that saved me from despair because my life was to become even rockier.

As you know, I practice astrology. My natal astrology chart is set up in a way suggesting lifelong shocks, and breakdowns can be seen in the planet placements of my chart. I believe my chart is a template for my chosen path to enlightenment, and boy did I choose a doozy! My chart suggests that until my soul is allowed to flourish through an open heart, certain bumps and upsets would function to jar me into awakening. I confess that the face plants I've experienced in life so far have certainly served to wake me up.

Around the age of four or five months, my family moved from California to Kansas where my father was to attend the United States Army Command and General Staff College. He left his position as camp commander at Camp Roberts in San Luis Obispo where he oversaw the decommissioning of soldiers returning from the Pacific Front. I was born during his tenure there in February of 1945.

Sometime in the spring of that year, he loaded the family up in our car for the move to Kansas. The tribe included my father and mother, my three-and-a-half-year-old brother, my aunt (who had traveled from South Carolina by train to help with the journey), and myself. Mom made a bed for me in the back seat, pinned a glamour shot of the actress Hedy Lamarr to the headliner above my travel bed (Mom claimed that I stared and smiled at the photo the entire trip), and along with our luggage, we set out to travel east.

Then tragedy struck. Mom told me the story decades later— that at some point we stopped in a small town for everyone to stretch legs and take a breather. Mom, Aunt Betty, and my brother were somewhere, probably the restroom, and I was left in the back seat with Dad watching me. The story is that Dad decided he needed something from one of the suitcases that made up my bed. He rearranged the bed on the back seat, took out the suitcase, and left the car for a moment to retrieve whatever he was looking for. In that brief time he had the suitcase out on the hood of the car, I managed to roll over and fall down into the space between the seat and the car door and suffocate.

It must have been during cool weather because the car windows were up, and Dad didn't hear anything. When Dad returned, I was lodged in that tiny space, not breathing, and had turned blue. Dad resuscitated me. Mom never elaborated on the story, and I can only imagine the scene when she arrived back from her bathroom break. Of course, I have no memory of this event but developed a lifelong inability to draw in enough air. I think it was related to this trauma. At one point, I took up yoga, and in those classes, learned how to breathe deeply once again.

In the Shamanic tradition of native peoples, it is believed that children who have died and come back to life make the best shamans. Here's a brief description of the term "shaman" taken from Wikipedia:

> *A shaman (/ˈʃɑːmən/ SHAH-men) is someone who is regarded as having access to, and influence in, the world of benevolent and malevolent spirits, who typically enters into a trance state during a ritual, and practices divination and healing.*[11]

I believe that my brush with death sensitized me to the world of the unseen and contributed to my abilities to trust the information that I was able to pick up from non-verbal communication. There are many traditions (not all of them life-threatening) that describe the process that goes into making someone super sensitive, and I'll leave it up to the reader to explore these traditions. It is a fascinating realm of information.

My history of trauma did not stop there. I'm amazed I survived childhood at all! When I was seven, I waded into a pack of dogs to rescue a cat they had trapped in a corner of our apartment building where we were living at the time. The cat bit me severely on the hand during the rescue attempt, but he did escape up a tree. However, I was gushing blood and went screaming home to Mom. She treated the wound with iodine, put a Band-Aid on it, and set me on my way. Within a few days, I developed terrible symptoms, one of which was sepsis. I was taken to the doctor where I was given a fifty-fifty chance of survival, shot with penicillin, and made to endure the rabies treatment. I was very sick for a long time. My grandmother, a nurse, came to the house daily to give me the injections.

When I was eleven, my family was staying in Newport Beach in a home owned by my father's boss. They were on a cruise, and we were house sitting. They had a pool in the backyard that was heated, and kids from the neighborhood often spent the day swimming. Everyone showered after swimming, so the hot water heater was set at its highest temperature, nearly boiling. The bathroom had a sliding glass tub enclosure, which was a new feature for me. On the day the family who owned the house was returning, my family planned a big BBQ party, and the place was filled with adults and children with everyone going in and out of the pool and the showers. I was excited, and when I finished my shower, I accidently turned off only the cold water tap—at that point, scalding hot water hit me. I panicked, fell in the tub, and proceeded to nearly boil myself. I finally got the water turned off just as my father broke down the bathroom door. A doctor arrived and administered enough morphine to distract me from the agony. It took months to recover from the first and second-degree burns on forty-five percent of my body.

The final assault I managed on my body happened at age fourteen when I broke my leg riding my friend's horse—sidesaddle without a saddle. After that, I stopped tempting fate so dramatically.

My history is unique in many ways. However, I believe we all choose our own path to awareness. My path seemed to require lots of jolts and close calls. I've taught people to be animal communicators whose lives were as peaceful and normal seeming as can be imagined. All that is required to develop the ability is a strong desire to do so.

ANIMALS IN DREAMS

Often dreams with animals in them can seem frightening. It's my belief that we are given these symbols in our sleeping state to open up our hearts to the need to integrate instinctual energies that have been disowned or denied. After my stepdaughter Lacey died recently, I dreamt of her visiting me with a wild jaguar. In my dream, she appeared at the large window in our foyer, the jaguar at her side, both looking at me with great intensity. The wind blew, and Lacey's long hair whipped around her face as she embraced the wild cat. Just as suddenly, they both vanished into the dream forest. I awoke and meditated on the dream, seeing it as a gift offering from her spirit. Jaguars are wild, predatory and beautiful. I believe Lacey was reminding me not to disown those qualities in myself and others.

Many decades ago, when I was in art school and enjoying my life to its fullest (i.e., partying), I dreamt I descended into a cellar in which lurked a large, silver wolf. Remember, wolves are pack animals. Wolf's appearance in your dreams is a reminder to carefully consider who you are "running" with. I did so, and soon after changed my residence and friends to facilitate a more creative and fulfilling life.

LEARNING FROM ANIMALS

I've found talking to animals to be one long, continuous learning curve. Nearly every week, I learn important spiritual lessons from animals whether in a session or a chance encounter—communications from animals that are teachings for me.

One of my earliest lessons came during my visit to Lexington with Blue, the Belgian mare I wrote about earlier. That brilliant white light she sent me was a blessing. She communicated a divine energy from her third eye directly to mine. The feeling of elation stayed with me for a long time and is easy to recall today. The experience taught me that animals have the ability to affect us strongly with their gratitude. I learned that animals are masters at directing divine energy towards others. The enormity of this revelation stays with me and continues to shape my thoughts about what it means to be human on this earth. Whenever someone sends you a blessing or prayer, it always appears in your body as a brilliant, divine healing light.

In my work I often see animals I consider "angels in fur suits." I don't know how that term originated. It just popped into my head one day as I worked with an animal that was clearly helping her human. Angels in fur suits are just that: angelic spirits that take animal form. These animals share advanced spiritual connections with their humans. If you have ever had such a relationship, you know what I'm talking about here.

An example I'll give is of a twenty-eight-year-old pony I met at SIRE many years ago. SIRE is a Houston-based therapy horse program currently with three locations. They brought me to Houston to do a fund-raiser, and in the course of the event, I was able to visit one of their facilities and talk with this very special pony. I've forgotten his name, but I will always remember his spirit. I was told that he was especially gifted at working with children with autism. When I talked with him, I asked him how he was able to help the children. He told me, and also showed me, how while a child was on his back, he would bring energy up from the earth in spirals around his four legs and then spiral the earth energy up around the child, connecting the child with the calming energies of Mother Earth. Combined with the fun and relaxation the children felt when they rode him, the energies accelerated their development by grounding them and helping them feel more comfortable in their bodies. This little wise soul of a pony is what I consider a shamanic being, a healer of the highest order. He had been working with children all of his life, and in his retirement, he was doing his most profound work.

A more recent learning experience occurred while working with Oliver, a young eleven-month-old cat having trouble getting settled into his new forever home. His person was concerned that Oliver was not fitting in. Her two-year-old cat Lola was confrontational with Oliver and screaming at him for minor infractions such as inappropriate tail sniffing and the like. Lola, in our communication, told me that Oliver had atrocious manners (true—all kittens need to learn their manners!). My client didn't understand that until Lola got Oliver under her control she was having none of his nonsense. The other cat, Churro, a friendly five-year-old, wanted to be Oliver's friend but didn't know how to relate with him because Oliver hadn't settled in and was skittish. Oliver wouldn't even go into the family room. My human client was understandably upset with all the drama, and I assured her there was nothing out of the ordinary happening. They just needed time to adjust.

I worked with Oliver's energy, smoothing out the tension that had bunched up in the third (processing information and general digestion) chakra, helping him appreciate that he's in his forever home and that everyone was there to help him adjust. As I felt Oliver relax, I noticed that he started shooting threads of energy out of his compassion chakra. That's the minor chakra located between the heart and the throat. It's the chakra that helps all beings communicate compassion and love. When it's open, your thoughts and words come through as supportive to yourself and to others. Oliver was suddenly showering the room with the energy of compassion for himself! Cats are master energy workers and are masters at feng shui. They will come into a room and attach themselves energetically to objects as a way to ground their experience. However, I had never witnessed this behavior in action before, and watching Oliver do it astounded me. I realize that the energy cats use for this behavior comes from compassion for the self. It shows a great deal of trust in their environment.

My all-time favorite discovery came as the answer to the great cat mystery: How is it that cats can seemingly "float" from a lower surface to a higher surface? After observing my feline friends for years, I learned that they had the ability to "shoot" energy across distances, anchor it, and then follow it to get to where they wanted to go. Many years before, I witnessed Buster shoot energy up to a counter high above him and then float up to the counter on the energy he had created. But I had not seen where in his body that energy emerged. I think human athletes can do this and call the skill "being in the zone." I think their "intention" shoots the energy gathered from being in the zone to the desired goal and then they simply let everything follow from there. Of all my amazing discoveries practicing animal communication, this is right up there as among the most exciting.

IN THE REALM OF FRIENDS AND STRANGERS IN SPIRIT: ANIMAL COMMUNICATION AS A GATEWAY TO THE WORLD OF SPIRIT

By now it should be clear that humans are capable of receiving information from unknown realms. I have no explanation about where the information that comes to me originates. It's a deep and abiding mystery, and I suspect it should remain so. That said, I'm intensely curious, and I see that science has lately been writing about successful experiments in which information can be present at two locations simultaneously. It's called "non-locality." Perhaps something like it explains how I can know something that is going on in another part of the world. But like I said, it's all very strange and wonderful, and I don't for a second pretend to understand why it works. For me, it's like breathing. I don't really understand the mechanisms of breath—I just trust the process. Luckily I was raised in an environment that supported my creativity and my imagination. No one ever told me that my connection with and ability to communicate with other species was nonsense.

I had a great imagination and was loved for it by my family. I remember feeling so proud when I heard the adults talk about how wonderful my imagination was for them. I had an enlightened public school education in Southern California, which had the best school system in the country back in the day when education was given strong national and regional support. My mind was shaped and guided by some of the best teachers in the country, and I seldom felt judged or rejected. My spiritual education was also rich. I was required to go to church, and I came away from that experience with an appreciation that we as humans need a belief system that acknowledges a divine presence in the universe.

I had a wonderful aunt who told me her own original stories at bedtime—creative, weird, and wonderful stories about a panda that could ride moonbeams up into space and have amazing inter-planetary adventures. As she spun her tale, I held the little stuffed panda that had belonged to my father as a child, and I snuggled deeper into the quilts. I loved her stories about that magical bear, and hearing them cultivated my enjoyment of writing. Enlight-ened education, spirituality, and encouragement to enjoy and develop creativity and imagination were among the best things I took from my complicated childhood.

As I grew up, I learned that there is tremendous power in the world of spirit. I find that the power is for good and can only be accessed through a loving heart. I know there are stories galore of evil powers but these stories only talk about a certain type of power: The power that fear has over us. I believe the world can be a benevolent experience once we master our own fear by learning to act with courage. It takes courage to face life at its most difficult and emerge with your faith in goodness intact. Cynicism and defeat result, in my experience, from the collapse of courage.

Animals are very courageous by nature. They will defend themselves when attacked. They will find food and shelter if alone. They raise families in the wild on instinct alone. Domestic animals often don't need to rely on instinct as their human guardians feed, nurture, and protect them. However, when a cat gets lost, her instincts will take over. When a dog is lost, he'll work hard to find shelter and safety.

Animals have taught me many life lessons. I listen to them and know I can trust their wisdom. Working with dying animals helped me face and overcome my own fear of death. When I work with dying animals, they show me how they leave the body and return to their ancestors for a celebration. Dogs in spirit will celebrate with a run with their ancestral pack, and cats often love to return to their favorite spaces and meditate or hang out in a sunny space.

Years ago, I had a lucid dream in which I met my deceased cat Buster I in spirit. In the dream, he was among a large group of cats, all in meditative poses (which I call the "basic meatloaf" pose), in the sanctuary of a beautiful modern church situated in a lush forest. I was thrilled to see Buster I again. In the dream, I picked him up and began walking to the exit, holding him in my arms. It was then that I heard a booming voice overhead asking, "What are you doing?" to which I replied, "Taking Buster I home." The voice then said to me, "You can't. He's dead." I woke up abruptly from that dream and have meditated on it since. There is a veil, and for a given incarnation, death is final. However, it is possible to visit the dead, taking with you the respect necessary to navigate the journey.

When we moved into our home thirteen years ago, my husband, myself, and our cats all started to encounter a large long-haired white cat in spirit. I first saw him one late afternoon, around dusk, while I was coming up the stairs. From the landing, I saw him jump from the fireplace hearth and run under the sofa in the living room—as if startled by my appearance. I thought it might be Buster, so I looked under the sofa, and there was no one there. I found Buster sleeping peacefully on the bed. I mentioned this to Hans, and he told me he'd seen the cat too. He just forgot to tell me! Then I started noticing the cats would stare up to the landing at the top of the stairs when we were all watching TV in the media room downstairs. Buster, Peaches, and even Bear would hang out with us, and all of them kept watching the landing. I realized our cat spirit was hanging out there in the evening during our TV hour, also keeping a watchful eye on us.

Fast forward a year or so, and I take Buster in for a routine checkup with his divine vet, whose name happens to be Angel. I'd gotten to know Angel better and knew I could be open with her about my abilities, so I shared my story about the cat spirit in our home. Then Angel told me something that really amazed me: She had grown up with one of the girls whose family owned the home before us. The mom had a big white cat that had died suddenly from a stroke in the home a few years before we purchased it. I realized we had a friend in spirit living with us. This cat stayed with us for about ten years and then decided to move on. We had moved in with five adult cats, but over the years, they all went to spirit, and when Buster went to spirit in 2014 our ghost cat joined him and has not been seen since.

Sometime during the fifth year of my practice, I began to experience people without bodies (in spirit) visiting me during my animal communication sessions. The first experience was as startling as it was unexpected. I was on the phone helping a man from Florida with a dog he had just rescued from a busy street in his hometown. The dog had been running down the landscaped median and was in danger of being hit by a car as he dashed in and out of traffic. My client stopped his car, opened the door, and the dog jumped into the back seat. He brought the dog home, and my client called me to see if the dog would tell me his story.

During our consultation, a very jolly fat man popped into my field of psychic vision. I use the term "psychic vision" to refer to what I "see" in my mind's eye during a consultation. The man introduced himself as George and told me he wanted to speak to my client, Mark. I interrupted my dialogue concerning the lost dog and asked Mark if he knew a fat, jolly man named George. There was a significant pause on the other end of the line and then Mark said, "George is my father's name. He just passed away a few months ago."

Mark, George, and I continued to have a remarkable conversation. George was humorous, pleasant, caring, and kind beyond words. George had wanted to speak to all of his family members, and I did eventually receive calls from his wife and adult children who were scattered all over the country. George was extremely generous of spirit, and his visits lifted everyone. I eventually became good friends with his wife, and she sponsored a few workshops in her hometown in Texas.

I grew up flying in my dad's airplanes, and even though we often experienced turbulence, and once were in a fairly dangerous situation, I never feared flying. For me, getting into a little private airplane to travel was the height of joy and adventure. There is a thrill to flying that can't be duplicated by any other activity. We soared high above the ground for hours back in the day with no electronics or other distractions (I got airsick if I read). The interiors of those little single-engine planes were cramped and noisy. The vibrations and roar of the engine put me into an altered state, and my imagination took flight. My brother and I—crammed into the little back seat—made up incredible stories, usually involving space travel. We'd be on distant planets having grand adventures.

I remember flying over this great land at a time when light pollution did not exist in most parts of the country. Night flying with a full moon under an inky sky, looking down to the earth lit only by an occasional small town, ranch light, or string of lights along a highway is a treat no longer possible. When we flew during the new moon, the stars of the Milky Way were so bright that my young mind could barely contain the awe of the vision. My memories of these experiences still fill me with wonder.

As I've written earlier, my father died in 1960 when the plane he was flying collided midair with a Navy Trainer. The occupants of the Navy Trainer landed safely, but my father died that day. I was fifteen when my father's accident happened. My brain was not developed enough to take in the scope of the tragedy, and I was deeply scarred. My brother grieved the loss of his father, but he eventually healed and went on to have a successful life. As time went on, my mother moved from California back to her home state of South Carolina, remarried, and had a successful second marriage. I, however, was left adrift in my teenage years. Back then there was no grief counseling to speak of; just suck it up and move on with your life. One of the great casualties of this period was my love of flying. I never again enjoyed it and even developed a phobia around travel by plane.

Then George enters my life forty-one years later. By this time I'd been the intermediary between George and his entire family, and I'd gotten to really adore him. On a trip returning from Houston, Texas, where I had been the animal communicator in residence at the annual Pin Oak Charity Horse Show, I sat on the plane, buckled up and ready for takeoff. I was in my usual state of dread. I should have been feeling elated over the fun I'd had at the show. I wasn't; I was feeling the anxiety that always accompanied me when flying. Suddenly, George shows up and I can "see" him clearly sitting next to me in the seat that was mercifully empty. George explained that his job in life had taken him around the world and that he was constantly in the air travelling. He assured me that I would be safe and that there was nothing to fear. I felt him holding my hand and comforting me. Tears came to my eyes as my heart opened. I felt his assurance and love so completely in that moment that I haven't feared flying since.

I haven't heard from George in many years but know that he's one of the great spirits in the world of unseen beings in spirit. Did George know that my plane would land safely? I don't think that was the point. I believe George was communicating to me from a place where there is nothing to be afraid of, a place of love, a place we're all headed. I think he wanted to share this enormous peace with me.

I'll return here to the story of my meeting with Chief Two Trees, which I began at the beginning of this book. This story is about Chief's first teaching to me. He was generous with his teachings, and I was later to find out he had many students from around the world that he mentored.

When Chief Two Trees arrived at my office that late spring day, I was having a particularly difficult time with what I had for years felt was a haunting by my father's spirit. I knew that my father was not at peace, and since his accident, he had visited me often in a state of agitation. I was a teenager, and his antics scared me. Movies such as *Poltergeist* and *The Exorcist* were not going to be frightening teenagers for a few decades to come. I was isolated and dealing with these issues alone—telling no one. But at the time of Chief's visit to my office in the mid 1990s, I was experiencing one of those visitations. This visitation was different, however, in that Dad's spirit appeared to me for the first time as silent and stone-grey in color. He was accompanied by what I perceived to be a guardian angel even though I hadn't thought of guardian angels since the prayers of my childhood. I didn't drink much or consume recreational drugs nor was I on any prescription drugs. My mind was creating this experience out of the blue—I didn't think I was crazy either; after all, I worked full-time, enjoyed friends, had two cats, and had a wonderful daughter in college. My life seemed okay and within the boundaries of normal.

As Chief sat opposite my desk, he silently stared at me, his big eyes full of compassion. He seemed relaxed and fully present at the same time, and he put me at ease in spite of my earlier fears of his powers. I found myself opening up to him as though he were my best friend. I told him the story of my father's accident, his spirit visits, of his grey, silent presence and of the "guardian angel" that acted as his interpreter. I told him about the stories the angel was telling me of my father's life, his mistakes, his regrets, and his sorrows. It was all very disturbing to me, but I could not stop myself. I was aware that my confession to Chief would be interpreted as complete fabrication. The story I heard myself telling seemed unreal even to me. Chief sat there in total calm and acceptance. When I was done spilling this tale to him, I was quite upset. This was not the kind of story you'd tell a stranger, especially one that had powers that were beyond my understanding.

Chief Two Trees then spoke to me, quietly and with a dignity that assured me that he had appreciated every word I had uttered. He told me that what I was seeing was my father's Mineral Spirit, and the guardian angel was his spirit guide. Chief went on to say that, according to Cherokee beliefs, all beings have three spirits—animal, vegetable, and mineral. When a being dies violently, often their Mineral Spirit is left at the scene of death and cannot leave the Earth. He said I needed to do a ceremony to release my father's Mineral Spirit, which was trapped in the Earthly realm. Our entire exchange lasted no more than thirty minutes and then Chief quietly left my office.

Exhausted, I packed up and went home for the weekend. I contacted a friend, a man who had been a Catholic priest but who had quit to marry the love of his life. I told my friend about the encounter with Chief Two Trees and asked if he would help with designing a ritual to release my father's Mineral Spirit. My friend obliged, and later in the week, we met to release my father. Many years passed after that experience, and I heard no more about my father. I didn't even dream about him. Then one night in early 2008, I had a dream in which I walked outside my home and saw my father looking like the handsome young man he had once been, leaning against the wall of my carport. I was surprised and asked him what he was doing there. He replied, "I am here to help you." And he has. His strength has been available to me whenever I've needed it.

As I have written earlier, animals do not always know they're deceased. Chief gave me my first lesson in the complexities of spirit life. If an animal has died suddenly and or violently, their spirit often continues on as if embodied, just as my father's mineral body had stayed close to me. The big white cat that haunted our home in North Carolina had died in such a way and was hanging out until the time was right for him to return to his ancestors. When I work with lost animals, I have to be aware of this possibility and let the client know that the world of spirit is complex, and I am still learning. My clients agree to work with me because they know I am good at my job and there's established trust. However, as I have stated before, I still make mistakes. That's how I know I'm still learning and probably will be till I leave this body I now possess.

CHARLESTON AND ITS LOST SOULS

Shortly after George's visit, I began to see spirits turn up regularly in my animal communication practice. I was living on Sullivan's Island, South Carolina where, in the days of slavery, victims were brought by slave ships and deposited in quarantine until cleared of any disease they may have contracted on the ship. Many of these poor souls perished under horrid conditions, and their souls still haunt the Charleston area. Others died by violence, hanging, or beatings. Still others died in the periodic pestilence common in that period. Living in Charleston as an empath could be difficult at times because of these hauntings.

The following story is a good example of the work I've done with clients in Charleston, South Carolina whose animal friends have been disturbed by the anguished spirits of the people who have perished in tragic circumstances. Kay Newman lives in a beautiful, fashionable neighborhood south of Broad on the Charleston Peninsula. She contacted me about a problem she was having with her cats. Here are her words about the extraordinary session that followed:

Our four-year-old cats, Max and Lola, who are loving best friends and littermates, were very uncharacteristically fighting. To be more specific, Lola, the beautiful female, was viciously attacking her twenty-four-pound brother! She was hissing and making high-pitched noises, screeching at him and swiping at him. Fur was flying, and it seemed like a battle to the death. It was disturbing to all of us to hear and witness. And oddly, my husband noted that these attacks were only taking place on the first floor of our home, never on the second floor.

We finally took them both to our vet because we were so undone by Lola's behavior. The vet said that they seemed very healthy. Then she asked if we lived in an old house. In fact, we do live in the South of Broad neighborhood in Charleston, SC. Our 1910 home was built on a landfill, and the original seawall runs just behind our house—two blocks from the low battery and Charleston Harbor.

The vet offered that she thought we might have a ghost. She was a bit shy about suggesting it, but also said she had seen it many times in her years of practice in Charleston. She suggested that I call Diane Samsel. I told Diane that our vet suggested that I call her. I made suggestions that perhaps there was some energy of soldiers or maybe simply another animal outside that was upsetting Lola.

Over the phone (she's in NC) Diane said, "Let me take a look. . . ." And she was quiet for a few minutes. She asked if our house was in a field or had an open space around it, and I explained how it had been marsh before it was filled. Then she started to make the sound R—"Rrrrr." Then she said, "Rufus." She explained that Rufus was an enslaved African and had been hanged on a tree on the site of our house when it was still marsh and that his spirit had not been able to leave. He had stayed with the tree and had been there for a long time.

Then Diane asked if anything really good had happened in our house recently. It was exactly the opposite—I had been hospitalized in the intensive care unit for a very severe trauma and had experienced significant blood loss. Many people had sent out their very positive thoughts and prayers for my recovery. Diane said that the positive energy had woken Rufus, and he was lonely—so he had been trying to take our male cat, Max, as his companion. The female cat, who was clearly more sensitive to this, was not attacking her brother but trying to defend him from Rufus.

Then Diane went quiet for a bit, again, and said, "Look, he is showing me his ship that he came over on." She was speaking with great reverence, and I joined her in that feeling. It seemed clear to both of us that something special was happening.

Then she was silent another moment or so. Then "Oh, look! There is a beautiful, feminine energy—mother energy—coming for him. They are showing me their village in Africa, which is beautiful and full of loving people. She is taking him back there." I asked, "Can I help? Can we help them?" Diane said, "Wish them well—wish them back there." Which I did. It was as if I could feel that maternal energy. I wanted to join and help.

More moments of silence followed. Then Diane said, "Look, he's coming back—oh, he's coming back to get the tree!" And then she said, "He is gone."

We both were silent for a good while. It felt to me like we had just been a part of something sacred. I said this to Diane, and she said it was a wonderful experience for her as well.

She told me that the reason that Lola was attacking Max was because Rufus was attracted to Max's big personality and his energy. Lola could see Rufus's energy around Max, and she was not actually attacking Max but attacking the energy she could see around Max that was coming from Rufus. Rufus, she said, had been lonely for many, many years, and he wanted Max as a playmate. She said that Rufus was not a bad guy and that he was not guilty of whatever he was charged with and shouldn't have been hanged. He needed the original energy from the prayers and then our focused energy to help him. Rufus's energy wasn't [able] *to get to the second floor of the house, only on the first floor.*

From the moment Diane said, "He is gone." There have been no further catfights on the first floor of our house, and that was five years ago.

Working with spirit has a rewarding side: healing. It is possible to help people and their animals move beyond painful grief with the power of communication and dialogue. When I listen with an open heart and mind, I can be present to the pain expressed by the mourner. Taking in another's pain requires compassion, an emotion that is a part of the healing process. Grieving people need a lot of compassion.

THE TRAGEDY OF BACKYARD BREEDING, PUPPY/KITTEN MILLS

Abuse of animals breaks the heart. A civilization can be judged on how well it treats animals. Outstanding people such as Dr. Temple Grandin[12] have given the twenty-first century solid, scientific grounds for treating animals humanely. Many groups have formed to fight animal abuse on all levels. Because my clients are caring animal guardians, I do not deal with heartbreaking abuse. If an abused animal has come into the home of a caring human, that person is going to do everything possible to heal the wounds the animal has suffered. I do my part to help animals in peril, often volunteering my services for fund-raisers for rescue groups. It's a service I enjoy tremendously. I also donate money. What I don't do is donate my service as an animal communicator to individuals or groups to work one-on-one with an animal. Early in my career I tried it but came to realize it would be an endless task, leaving me no time to build a consulting practice.

When people innocently purchase a purebred dog from a pet store or a breeder, they run the risk of ending up with an animal that has catastrophic genetic and/or emotional dysfunction. America has very lax standards when it comes to registered purebred animals for sale in the pet industry. There are groups in the Midwest who run some of the most notorious breeding facilities where dogs are kept in crowded, filthy cages, and the bitches are bred to exhaustion and suffer gestation and birth in cramped, unhealthy conditions. Cats are bred in tiny cages in dark buildings under similar conditions. America fosters a factory farm mentality towards animals in which the pursuit of profit puts animals at extreme risk.

In England, by contrast, breeding standards are very strict to ensure a healthy animal. People will go to the trouble to import their puppies from abroad to ensure a healthy dog. Unfortunately, I purchased my Siberian husky, Sara, from a backyard breeder who didn't know what she was doing. I didn't know what I was doing either. Lacey had wanted to adopt a husky, and when I took her to pick out a pup, I saw Sara and fell in love. At the time, I was ignorant of such things myself. Sara had a congenital kidney defect, which I did not discover until months after I had recovered her from her abduction ordeal. At about the age of two, she began peeing every hour and sometimes could not hold her urine. She began to lose weight. I took her to the vet and discovered her kidneys had not grown to adult size and that she was in renal failure. It was with a broken heart that I ended up having her euthanized as she could no longer eat or walk. The ordeal served as a wakeup call. Several years after I became a communicator, I began to appreciate how much education is needed to upgrade our relationship with the animal kingdom.

I have worked with a number of clients who buy little toy breeds from unscrupulous breeders only to find they have a beloved friend with a host of terrible health and behavior problems that develop quickly. These kind guardians must nurse sick puppies back to health. Sometimes they fail to do so, and the results are tragic.

Some heartless breeders dump unwanted animals onto the streets or into rescue groups, and when I talk to these animals, their stories are horrible. I recently talked with a male small breed dog that had been so deprived of basic comfort, decent food, and socialization that he was both physically damaged beyond salvation and in a state of near psychosis. After a few traumatic conversations, the little dog's person concluded the humane thing to do would be to put the little soul out of its misery. I agree with such choices in these circumstances. Animals, as I have said, live closer to the world of spirit and have little fear of death as it doesn't occur to them that life ever ends. But it is our responsibility to limit the amount of suffering they have to endure under our care.

KEEPING OUR FRIENDS HEALTHY

When illness is too advanced in an animal, the animal will prepare to leave the body. It's a process all creatures handle instinctively, knowing what to do. For instance, we once lived on three acres in Cincinnati, Ohio. Our street was a cul-de-sac, and there were no coyote packs in the vicinity, so our cats enjoyed the outdoors.

We had known for some time that Serena, our elderly cat, was preparing for her death when she disappeared into the woods on our property one day. Knowing she was looking to die naturally connected to the earth, or call forth a predator for a quick ending, I panicked. I wanted to say goodbye to her.

She had been suffering from cancer, and we knew her time was approaching fast. She didn't want treatment and was not afraid of leaving her body. I reached out intuitively to her and negotiated for her return. It took a few days as she was determined to do things her way. Serena had always been independent, having little use for humans. She was almost feral. Finally, she agreed that it would be best for me to help her cross so that I would be with her and the other animals in the house could mourn her passing. She was close to our other cats. She guided me, and I found her tucked up beneath the deck of our home in a place so hidden that I had to get up under the deck with a flashlight to see her. With her permission, I took her to the vet for euthanasia. She had a peaceful passing, and I was able to bury her body in her beloved hunting grounds, next to Sara's grave.

I am not trained in any healing modality. I use alternative healing practitioners for my own health maintenance and for the animals. I will use allopathic medicine for routine checkups and for health problems when nothing else is available. I lost my beloved aunt to cancer because she refused to see a medical doctor. She believed that her chiropractor could cure her, and she ended up dying prematurely, much to my sorrow.

If disease does strike, it's important to have a good medical diagnosis and then I believe in addressing underlying issues that created the disease. I was diagnosed with a goiter years ago. My mother had the same diagnosis when she was my age, and I knew it was probably a genetic issue. I went to a top specialist for a biopsy, consultation, and prognosis. It was not cancer, so I felt confident that I could address the problem with alternative medicine. Although my specialist strongly recommended surgery, I declined. There was a 10 percent or greater chance I'd die of complications, a 10 percent chance I'd lose my voice, and other risks.

I contacted a naturopath/homeopathist in Texas who specializes in treating thyroid issues with dietary and lifestyle changes, supplements, and homeopathic remedies. He was willing to do phone consultations. We worked together for several years, and my goiter, much to my excitement, slowly disappeared. But what's most important is that the fundamental body issues that created the goiter as a symptom were addressed and also pretty much healed. I feel much better now, have no scars and feel confident the goiter won't return. I am now working with him using my genetic profile from 23andMe. He has me on a protocol that addresses my genetic weaknesses. The hope is that I will not develop issues in the future that may arise from damaged chromosomes in my body. Veterinarians in some parts of this country offer this service for their animal patients!

Good health seems to boil down to the right genetics and the right strategies for maintaining health. And so it is with our animal friends' health. Here are some strategies and tips that I've found helpful:

CHEMICAL FREE

A friend of mine, an MD who specializes in treating breast cancer through prevention, says that at the cancer symposiums she attends, the consensus is that the prevalence of toxic chemicals in the environment is at the heart of the cancer epidemic. I recommend her book *Waking the Warrior Goddess* by Christine Horner, MD, FACS.[13] A clean, chemical-free environment seems to be essential when combating disease.

It's important to use cleaning materials that are organic and free of chemicals. I use water and vinegar on my floors and organic laundry detergent for my clothes. My makeup is all-natural as are my shampoo and bath products. I do this for my personal health but also to reduce the likelihood of our animal friends coming into contact with chemical residue.

If you have a lawn and are currently using chemicals, switch to organic. I use Gardens Alive! products and have for decades.

If you have carpets, clean them with non-toxic cleansers. I use OxiClean and hot water in a little hand-held carpet steamer on my rugs, and it works well. Check out a small section of your carpet first though. Most grocery stores now carry a selection of all-natural or organic cleaning products.

Cats don't enjoy the artificial scents in litter, so buy the un-scented product. And like the cat earlier in this book thought, artificial scents used in households to mask orders are just wrong! Candles and plugins are big offenders. Also to be avoided are the chemical products for spraying on surfaces to manage odor.

For odors, we use a formula given to us by a friend who is a dresser for a large ballet group: Mix one part water, one part cheap vodka, and lavender oil drops. We spray down our clothes, beds, curtains, and carpets with this mixture and it keeps the house fresh. And it's much more affordable than the toxic commercial products. We also use a diffuser with lavender oil for cleansing the air of bacteria, mold, and mildew.

HEALTHY DIET

I believe in species-appropriate diets as the foundation for good health for our animal friends, and as you might expect, "chemi-cal-free" applies to diet as well.

I developed an all-natural pet food supplement in the early 1980s that would eventually be named Power Paws. I moved to Houston, Texas at the end of the '70s and after living in that sub-tropical climate noticed my cats were shedding tremendous amounts of fur. Even though I had lived in the Southeast for over a decade at that point, I realized Houston heat and humidity was in a class of its own. Air conditioning could not keep up with it. I did a bit of research and created a powdered formula that could be sprinkled on the dry food I fed them at the time. After a few weeks, the shedding lessened noticeably, and their fur began to look a lot glossier.

Fast forward to the mid-1980s when my husband's work took us to Cincinnati, Ohio. My beloved aunt Dorothy Tennessee Samsel passed away and left me a small legacy. I invested that money in bringing my formula to market. The name Power Pets was not available, so I chose Power Paws and trademarked that name for my product. I designed a logo then mixed up my first large batch in my basement and began to market it around town. I enjoyed taking Power Paws to pet stores, health food stores, vet offices, and making pitches to companies such as Tree of Life in Bloomington, Indiana. I now license the formula to Gardens Alive! They sell it online and in their catalog under the name PetsAlive!

Choosing a species-appropriate diet is essential to maintaining your animal friend's health. For decades I fed a raw diet to my cats, and they thrived and lived long lives. When my cats aged significantly, I switched to a homemade crockpot diet developed by a veterinarian for my cats. Even through issues such as age-related kidney failure, I kept them on a clean diet, choosing not to use the "vet-approved" commercial diets. Commercial pet food manufacturers make generous corporate donations to veterinarian schools. Purina recently donated a new nutrition center to Louisiana State University School of Veterinary Medicine. I have a vet who does her own research, and she did not see proof that these diets are better than a clean, homemade, or very high-quality diet. I did adopt an older cat recently that will only eat kibble, so I feed him a grain-free brand made from organic and pasture-raised food sources.

The term "pasture-raised" refers to the practice of raising animals on living pasture as opposed to in cages or in buildings on bare earth, as cage-free implies. Pasture-raised animals, in addition to living in much more natural and humane conditions, are more nutritious. Pasture-fed cattle, for instance, are much more heart healthy for consumers. A web search of reputable sites suggests these benefits to eating cattle raised on grass:

Less total fat

More heart-healthy omega-3 fatty acids

More conjugated linoleic acid, a type of fat that's thought to reduce heart disease and cancer risks

More antioxidant vitamins, such as vitamin E

This approach to diet and health takes a bit more time and effort but is essential to the well-being of your animal friends. Animals fed in this way enjoy a healthier old age and spend less time at the vet.

When I began as an animal communicator, there were few options available, but today the healthy food market for cats and dogs is thriving. Dr. Karen Becker has a good book out on the subject: *Real Food for Healthy Dogs and Cats*.[14]

When your animal friend needs professional medical care, I recommend you check out the holistic vets in your community. In our small town, we take our cats to a clinic that offers chiropractic, acupuncture, herbal and alternative treatments, as well as traditional allopathic care.

CLOSING
THOUGHTS

*N*othing satisfies me more than happy clients, human and animal both. While finishing this book, I received a call that concluded a six-month journey that my client Jane took with her four-year-old Boykin Spaniel rescue, Jax. We had been working together since February, when Jax arrived rundown and suffering from heartworms. The treatment for heartworms takes a lot of time and is hard on the animal in many ways. Jax and Jane formed a tight bond that saw Jax slowly regain his health and discover for the first time in his life security, belonging, and true partnership.

Yesterday's call was about adjusting the finer points of Jax's health issues, beginning with detoxing his organs from the harsh chemicals he'd had to ingest for his recovery. Jane had him on a homemade super healthy diet, and he could not have had better care. Our conversation during the thirty-minute session was warm, friendly, and full of the love that Jax and Jane felt for one another. I know that Jax will go on to enjoy a full and happy life thanks to Jane's commitment and love for him. We concluded the conversation with a few requests from Jax and a few questions from Jane. All issues were resolved, and I felt so happy for them both.

I often wonder if there could be a better job on Earth than mine. While it's true that I have had a few less than successful communications, on the whole, each session is a treasure. The work keeps my heart centered and keeps me focused on what really matters in life: our love and care for one another. At the end of each day, I shut down my computer, turn off the lights to my office, and walk upstairs to fix dinner. This makes for a perfect end to the day in my world.

If you're wondering if you can do what I do, the answer is yes! I've trained doctors, lawyers, engineers, artists, quilters, rescuers, mothers, fathers, children, businesspeople, a nuclear physicist, and the list could go on forever. The journey to learning to listen with an open heart is a healing journey. When the heart becomes the instrument that you trust most, you'll never be caught believing a lie or trusting a con. The truth will shine through in everything you do, and in the end, the universe will deliver to your door, free of charge, everything you have coming to you. I encourage you to begin the journey.

SUGGESTED READING

Below is my list of suggested reading in the order I mentioned them, followed by a list of recommended authors and then some other titles I think you'll enjoy:

The Journey

What the Animals Tell Me by Beatrice Lydecker

Post-Tribal Shamanism:
A New Look at the Old Ways by Kenn Day

The Fundamentals

The Power of Intention: Learning to Co-create
Your World Your Way by Wayne Dyer

Are We Smart Enough to Know How Smart Animals Are?
by Frans de Waal

Proof of Heaven by Dr. Eben Alexander

The Practice

Sherlock Bones, Tracer of Missing Pets by John Keane

Four Paws, Five Directions: A Guide to Chinese Medicine for Cats
and Dogs by Cheryl Schwartz, DVM

Tools and Techniques

Embracing Our Selves: The Voice Dialogue Manual
by Hal and Sidra Stone

The Astrological Thesaurus – Book 1: House Keywords
by Michael Munkasey

Spirituality, Life Hacks, and Observations on Life, the Universe, and Everything

Waking the Warrior Goddess: Dr. Christine Horner's Program to Protect Against & Fight Breast Cancer
by Christine Horner, MD, FACS

Dr. Becker's Real Food for Healthy Dogs and Cats
by Dr. Karen Becker

Authors:

Eben Alexander

Ted Andrews

Dr. Karen Shaw Becker and Beth Taylor

Carlos Castaneda

Kenn Day

Frans de Waal

Wayne Dyer

Dr. Temple Grandin

Christine Horner, MD, FACS

John Keane

Beatrice Lydecker

Diane Samsel

Michael Munkasey

Cheryl Schwartz

Penelope Smith

Hal and Sidra Stone

Noel Tyl

Other Recommended Books:

Animal Speak and Animal-Wise by Ted Andrews

Complementary and Alternative Veterinary Medicine: Principles and Practice by Allen M. Schoen DVM MS and Susan G. Wynn DVM

Animals in Spirit: Our Faithful Companions' Transition to the Afterlife by Penelope Smith

Mama's Last Hug: Animal Emotions and What They Tell Us about Ourselves by Frans de Waal

Embracing Your Inner Critic: Turning Self-Criticism into a Creative Asset by Hal and Sidra Stone

Synthesis & Counseling in Astrology: The Professional Manual by Noel Tyl

Thinking in Pictures: My Life with Autism by Dr. Temple Grandin. Also, for an enjoyable and informative introduction to Temple Grandin's life and contributions, I highly recommend the movie *Temple Grandin* produced by HBO Films and Ruby Films, 2010.

BIBLIOGRAPHY

Alexander, Eben. 2012. *Proof of Heaven: A Neurosurgeon's Journey into the Afterlife*. New York: Simon & Schuster.

n.d. *Astrolabe*. Accessed May 07, 2019. https://alabe.com/.

Day, Kenn. 2014. *Post-Tribal Shamanism: A New Look at the Old Ways*. Alresford: Moon Books.

de Waal, Frans. 2016. *Are We Smart Enough to Know How Smart Animals Are?* New York: W. W. Norton & Company, Inc.

n.d. *Dr. Temple Grandin's Website: Livestock Behaviour, Design of Facilities and Humane Slaughter*. Accessed May 11, 2019. http://www.grandin.com/.

Dyer, Wayne. 2004. *The Power of Intention: Learning to Co-Create Your World Your Way*. Carlsbad: Hay House, Inc.

Horner, M.D., F.A.C.S., Christine. 2013. *Waking the Warrior Goddess: Dr. Christine Horner's Program to Protect Against & Fight Breast Cancer*. 3rd. Laguna Beach: Basic Health Publications, Inc.

Keane, John. 1979. *Sherlock Bones, Tracer of Missing Pets*. Philadelphia: Lippincott Williams & Wilkins.

Lydecker, Beatrice. 1977. *What the Animals Tell Me*. New York: Harper & Row.

Munkasey, Michael. 1992. *The Astrological Thesaurus - Book 1: House Keywords.* St. Paul: Llewellyn Publications.

Schwartz, Cheryl. 1996. *Four Paws, Five Directions: A Guide to Chinese Medicine for Cats and Dogs.* Berkeley: Celestial Arts.

Stone, Hal, and Sidra Stone. 1989. *Embracing Our Selves: The Voice Dialogue Manual.* Novato: Nataraj Publishing.

Stowell, Lucile Samsel. 1977. *The sorting of Samsels: An alphabetical genealogy of the surnames Sampsel, Sampsell, Sampselle, Samsal, Samsel, Samsell, Samsil, Somsel.* Mercer Island: L.S. Stowell.

Taylor, Beth, and Karen Shaw Becker, DVM. 2015. *Dr Becker's Real Food For Healthy Dogs and Cats: Simple Homemade Food.* Fourth. Natural Pet Productions.

n.d. *Temple Grandin's Official Autism Website.* Accessed May 11, 2019. https://www.templegrandin.com/.

n.d. *Time Cycles Research.* Accessed May 07, 2019. https://timecycles.com/.

Tyl, Noel. 1994. *Synthesis & Counseling in Astrology: The Professional Manual.* Woodbury: Llewellyn Publications.

—. n.d. *www.noeltyl.com.* Accessed May 06, 2019. https://www.noeltyl.com/techniques/010530.html.

Wikipedia Contributors. n.d. *"Shamanism," Wikipedia, The Free Encyclopedia.* Accessed January 09, 2019. https://en.wikipedia.org/w/index.php?title=Shamanism&oldid=876059768.

ENDNOTES

1   Beatrice Lydecker, *What the Animals Tell Me* (New York: Harper & Row, 1977).

2   Frans de Waal, *Are We Smart Enough to Know How Smart Animals Are?* (New York: W. W. Norton & Company, Inc., 2016).

3   Eben Alexander, *Proof of Heaven: A Neurosurgeon's Journey into the Afterlife* (New York: Simon & Schuster, 2012).

4   Noel Tyl, See for instance: *Analytical Techniques: Management of Measurement Constructs—Reflections Upon the Moon*, accessed May 6, 2019, https://www.noeltyl.com/techniques/010530.html.

5   Lucile Samsel Stowell, *The sorting of Samsels: An alphabetical genealogy of the surnames Sampsel, Sampsell, Sampselle, Samsal, Samsel, Samsell, Samsil, Somsel* (Mercer Island: L.S. Stowell, 1977), 91.

6   Cheryl Schwartz, DVM, *Four Paws, Five Directions: A Guide to Chinese Medicine for Cats and Dogs* (Berkeley: Celestial Arts, 1996).

7   Hal Stone, PHD, and Sidra Stone, PHD, *Embracing Our Selves: The Voice Dialogue Manual* (Novato: Nataraj Publishing, 1989)

8   "Astrolabe", accessed May 7, 2019, http://alabe.com/freechart.

9 "Time Cycles Research", accessed May 7, 2019, https://timecycles.com/.

10 Michael Munkasey, *The Astrological Thesaurus – Book 1: House Keywords* (St. Paul: Llewellyn Publications, 1992).

11 Wikipedia contributors, "Shamanism," Wikipedia, The Free Encyclopedia, accessed January 9, 2019, https://en.wikipedia.org/w/index.php?title=Shamanism&oldid=876059768.

12 "Dr. Temple Grandin's Website: Livestock Behaviour, Design of Facilities and Humane Slaughter", accessed May 11, 2019, http://www.grandin.com/, Also, "Temple Grandin's Official Autism Website", accessed May 11, 2019, https://www.templegrandin.com/.

13 Christine Horner, *Waking the Warrior Goddess: Dr. Christine Horner's Program to Protect Against & Fight Breast Cancer* (Laguna Beach: Basic Health Publications, Inc., 2013).

14 Beth Taylor and Karen Shaw Becker, DVM., *Dr. Becker's Real Food For Healthy Dogs and Cats: Simple Homemade Food, Fourth Edition* (Natural Pet Productions, 2015).

Made in the USA
Monee, IL
14 November 2022

17758171R00125